THE QUR'AN

WHAT EVERYONE NEEDS TO KNOW®

THE QUR'AN

WHAT EVERYONE NEEDS TO KNOW®

JANE McAULIFFE

OXFORD
UNIVERSITY PRESS

OXFORD
UNIVERSITY PRESS

Oxford University Press is a department of the University of Oxford. It furthers the University's objective of excellence in research, scholarship, and education by publishing worldwide. Oxford is a registered trade mark of Oxford University Press in the UK and certain other countries.

"What Everyone Needs to Know" is a registered trademark of Oxford University Press.

Published in the United States of America by Oxford University Press
198 Madison Avenue, New York, NY 10016, United States of America.

Library of Congress Cataloging-in-Publication Data
Names: McAuliffe, Jane Dammen, author.
Title: The Qur'an : what everyone needs to know / Jane McAuliffe.
Description: New York : Oxford University Press, 2020. |
Includes bibliographical references and index.
Identifiers: LCCN 2019047325 (print) | LCCN 2019047326 (ebook) |
ISBN 9780190867683 (hardback) | ISBN 9780190867676 (paperback) |
ISBN 9780190867706 (epub)
Subjects: LCSH: Qur'an. | Islam.
Classification: LCC BP130 .M396 2020 (print) | LCC BP130 (ebook) |
DDC 297.1/2261—dc23
LC record available at https://lccn.loc.gov/2019047325
LC ebook record available at https://lccn.loc.gov/2019047326

1 3 5 7 9 8 6 4 2

Paperback printed by LSC Communications, United States of America
Hardback printed by Bridgeport National Bindery, Inc.,
United States of America

*For friends and colleagues, especially those at the Library of Congress,
Bryn Mawr College, Georgetown University, the University of
Toronto, Emory University, and Trinity Washington University*

CONTENTS

PREFACE   XIII
ACKNOWLEDGMENTS   XIX

PART I. THE BOOK AND WHY IT MATTERS

1. Origins   3

Where did the Qur'an come from?   3
Who is Muhammad? Did he write the Qur'an?   4
Why does the Qur'an carry that name?   7
How long did it take to finish the Qur'an?   8
Did Muhammad know anything about other religions?   10
What happened to the Qur'an after Muhammad died?   12

2. Structure   15

Does the Qur'an have different parts?   15
Why do people say that the Qur'an is hard to read?   18
Are some parts of the Qur'an more important than others?   19
Is the Qur'an poetry or prose or both?   21

3. Beliefs About   23

Why do Muslims say that the Qur'an is God's own word?   23

Who is Gabriel and what is his connection to the Qur'an?   24

Does the Qur'an talk about itself?   26

Do Muslims believe that the Qur'an existed from all eternity?   27

Are all Qur'ans exactly the same or do different Muslim groups have
different Qur'ans?   29

Why do Muslims take a shower before touching the Qur'an?   30

PART II. MAJOR MESSAGES AND THEMES

4. God and Creation   35

What does the Qur'an say about God?   35

Is the God of the Qur'an the same as the God of the Bible?   37

Does the Qur'an describe the creation of the world?   38

How does the Qur'an talk about the natural world?   40

What is the relation of human beings to God and to nature?   41

Are there angels and devils in the Qur'an?   43

What are jinn?   44

5. Revelation, Prophecy, and History   46

Why is Muhammad called both a prophet and a messenger?   46

What other prophets appear in the Qur'an?   47

Does the Qur'an mention historical events?   49

6. Behavior and Judgment   52

What does the Qur'an say about death and life after death?   52

Are there descriptions of Heaven and Hell?   54

Is it true that the Qur'an promises a Paradise of virgins?   56

Does the Qur'an contain commandments? Is it a law book?   57

Do people determine their behavior or does God?   59

If people sin, can they repent and be forgiven?   60

Does the Qur'an predict the end of the world? Who is the Antichrist?   62

7. Religious Requirements   64

Why do Muslims pray five times a day?   64

Does the Qur'an say that Muslims must fast for an entire month?   66

Is pilgrimage to Mecca mentioned in the Qur'an?   68

How important is charity and generosity to others?   70

8. Family, Social, and Religious Relations   72

What does the Qur'an say about love and marriage? About children?   72

If a person dies, who inherits his or her property?   75

Is there a concept of community in the Qur'an?   76

Does the Qur'an tell Muslims how to treat non-Muslims?   78

Can Muslims marry non-Muslims?   80

Are there Qur'anic passages about other religions?   81

PART III. EXPERIENCING BY SOUND, SIGHT, AND TOUCH

9. Recitation   89

How do Muslims study the Qur'an? What if they don't speak Arabic?   89

Why is the Qur'an always recited in Arabic?   91

Do some people become famous for recitation?   92

Are there advanced degrees in qur'anic studies as there are in biblical studies?   94

10. Ritual and Prayer 97

Is the Qur'an used in public worship? In other formal ceremonies?   97

What role does the Qur'an play in Islamic mysticism?   98

Can the Qur'an keep bad things from happening? Can it secure
blessings?   100

11. Manuscripts, Public Architecture, and Material Culture ... 103

How important is the Qur'an to art and architecture in the Muslim world? 103

Is there a tradition of calligraphy and illumination for the Qur'an?   104

Are verses of the Qur'an ever written on ordinary objects?   106

PART IV. INTERPRETATION, INFLUENCE, AND GLOBAL DIFFUSION

12. Interpretation 111

Can the Qur'an be interpreted?   111

What are hadith and are they part of the Qur'an?   114

Do certain verses in the Qur'an guide its interpretation?   115

Are there different schools of interpretation among Sunni Muslims?
Among Shi'i Muslims?   117

Who decides which interpretation is the right one?   119

Can anyone interpret the Qur'an or do you have to be an expert?   120

Are there modern and contemporary interpreters of the Qur'an?   122

13. Scholarship 125

How have non-Muslims studied the Qur'an?   125

Is the Qur'an ever studied as a literary rather than a religious text?   127

Is there a connection between the Qur'an and the Bible?   128

Has the Bible been used to understand the Qur'an?   130

14. Influence   132

How did the Qur'an shape Islamic philosophy and theology?   132

What is the relationship between the Shari'a and the Qur'an?   134

What is the connection between the Qur'an and contemporary science?   136

What role does the Qur'an play in Arabic literature? In the literatures
of other Muslim cultures?   137

15. Translation and Transmission   140

Are Muslims allowed to translate the Qur'an?   140

When was the Qur'an translated into European languages?   142

When was the Qur'an first printed?   143

When did the Qur'an arrive in America?   145

How has the Internet affected the teaching and transmission of the
Qur'an?   147

PART V. WHAT DOES THE QUR'AN SAY ABOUT . . . ?

What does the Qur'an say about women?   152

What does the Qur'an say about veiling and separation?   154

What does the Qur'an say about polygyny?   155

What does the Qur'an say about abortion and birth control?   157

What does the Qur'an say about circumcision and female genital
mutilation?   158

What does the Qur'an say about hetero- and homosexual relations?   160

What does the Qur'an say about domestic violence?   162

What does the Qur'an say about divorce?   164

What does the Qur'an say about food and fasting?   165

What does the Qur'an say about drinking and drugs?   167

What does the Qur'an say about jihad?   169

What does the Qur'an say about war and terrorism?   171

What does the Qur'an say about slavery?   173

What does the Qur'an say about martyrs?   174

What does the Qur'an say about peace?   176

What does the Qur'an say about government and politics?   177

What does the Qur'an say about democracy?   179

What does the Qur'an say about international relations?   181

What does the Qur'an say about environmentalism?   182

What does the Qur'an say about financial transactions?   184

What does the Qur'an say about justice?   186

What does the Qur'an say about punishment?   187

What does the Qur'an say about Jews?   189

What does the Qur'an say about Christians?   191

What does the Qur'an say about apostasy?   193

What does the Qur'an say about blasphemy?   194

What does the Qur'an say about religious tolerance?   197

RECOMMENDED READING   **201**

INDEX   **205**

PREFACE

Not long ago, I took yet another flight to Cairo, a city that has fascinated me since my first visit more than thirty years ago. The trip was prompted by an invitation from Dr. Ahmed Al-Tayeb, the Shaykh Al-Azhar, to speak at Al-Azhar University. Founded in 970 (more than a century before any European university), Cairo's Al-Azhar University has attracted students from all over the Muslim world for more than a millennium and has produced more religious scholars than any other such institution. Many have dubbed Al-Azhar "the Islamic Vatican" and its leader, the Shaykh Al-Azhar, "the Muslim Pope." While the comparison falls short on several counts—Islam has no ordained clergy or centralized hierarchy—it captures the prestige of both the university and its leader within the world of Sunni Islam.

Dr. Al-Tayeb had invited a group of people, most of whom were former heads of state from Europe, Central Asia, and the Middle East, to speak on the topic "Islam and the West: Diversity and Integration." He also invited a few scholars, some from nearby universities and some from far away, to join the conversation and to provide insights from the university worlds that they represent. I was the only American among that handful of scholars, so I spoke about Islam in the United States and Canada, about how it is studied in our academic institutions, and about how American interest in Islam has skyrocketed in recent decades.

The return flight from Cairo to my home in Washington, D.C., provided time for reflection on all that has changed since my first trip there—and on all that has remained the same. Certainly the streetscape has shifted significantly, with much more traffic and pollution and many more women in head coverings and even face veils. Demographers will tell you that Cairo ranks among the world's fastest-growing cities and that its burgeoning population puts it on track to become one of the most congested urban areas on the planet. Yet much endures: the culture of coffee shops and intellectual salons; the labyrinthine bazaars and open-air markets; the myriad bookstores, large and small, offering just about everything published in the Arabic-speaking world; and the whole institutional infrastructure of a major Muslim city. Cairo's mosques and minarets span the centuries of Islamic architectural achievement. Its libraries and museums house an immense heritage, manuscripts dating back to the earliest periods of Islamic history. Its institutes and universities draw students from across the globe and educate religious leaders who serve not just in Egypt but in many other countries, as well. And over it all floats the five-time daily call to prayer, its evocative sounds reverberating from one loudspeaker to another across this vast metropolitan area.

I also thought about how well the conference topic, Islam and the West, suited the city that had hosted it. For centuries, Cairo has been a crossroads, as merchants, travelers, soldiers, and seekers thronged its streets and then stayed to shape its history. Facing to the East and to the West, with a history that subsumes both military occupation and peaceful settlement, the city now presents itself as a premier cosmopolitan center of the Muslim world. But it's a cosmopolitan center that suffers. The dashed hopes of the Arab Spring, subsequent authoritarian restrictions, terrorist attacks against both Muslims and

Christians: all have combined to severely damage the city's—
and the country's—economic and social stability.

It is against this recent background that Muslim religious
leaders came together in Cairo to convene an ongoing dialogue between the world of Islam and the world of the West.
What they did—and what they will continue to do—mirrors
efforts in North America, Europe, and elsewhere.

The connectivity fostered by globalization, coupled with the
increased tension generated by the tragedies of September 11
and other terrorist atrocities, has created an intellectual hunger
on both sides of the divide between the West and the Islamic
world. Americans, Europeans, and others in "the West" want
adequate and reliable information about Islam and the Muslim
world. But what they get is often misleading, distorted, and
sensationalized. To offset this, those of us who know something about these subjects have been working overtime to correct the inaccuracies and to stop the flow of misinformation.

Many religious leaders and scholars in the Muslim world
are on a similar quest. They want to know how people in
non-Muslim countries learn about Islam, the Qur'an, and the
fundamentals of Muslim faith and practice because they, too,
are fully aware of the falsehoods and fabrications that often
pass for the truth in many American and European media
outlets, whether news media or social media. Even more urgently, they seek to present a counternarrative to the perverse
and corrupted versions of Islam preached by groups like the
Taliban, Al-Qaeda, ISIS, and Boko Haram. I hope this book will
be helpful in their efforts.

All of my professional life, both Muslims and non-Muslims
have quizzed me about why I chose to focus my doctoral
studies and subsequent research and teaching on Islam and
the Qur'an. For many Muslims, this can present a doctrinal
difficulty. It's a point of faith that if someone comes to really know and understand the religion of Islam, its obvious
truth will prompt conversion. Trying to explain my fascina-
tion with Islamic thought and culture or to express a more

generalized interest in human religious experience usually
doesn't work very well as a response. Yet my initial interest
in the study of Islam grew out of just such motivations. As a
young graduate student, one who had spent all her earlier
years in Catholic schools, I was very curious about other religious traditions and about the philosophical questions generated by the encounter of those traditions, such as Islam and
Christianity, that make universalistic claims, that see themselves as the final truth, the fulfillment of the divine-human
encounter.

As my studies progressed and I became more immersed in
the primary sources (chiefly Arabic and Persian) of Muslim religious thought, I found myself sweeping back and forth between the extremes of familiarity and bewilderment. Much of
what I was learning echoed teachings and topics familiar from
my own religious tradition, but much else did not. Over and
over, I was both struck by Islam's similarities with Christianity
and Judaism and intrigued by the differences. Through all
those years of graduate school and then initial academic ap-
pointments, my study of Islam and the Qur'an could be considered an interesting historical and textual exploration, one
that allowed me to introduce students and audiences to an important part of human culture. In those earlier years, it never
occurred to me that understanding Islam and the Muslim
world would become a matter of national and international
consequence. Or that it would be a source of such sadness. In
recent years, news of heinous actions committed in the name
of Islam has appeared with depressing regularity. Despite the
efforts of Muslim religious leaders to denounce these events,
the association of "Islam" and "terrorism" has seeped deeply
into popular consciousness.

Finally, a more personal memory that will remain with me
from that conference in Cairo was the experience of being a
woman in that setting and on that stage. Not surprisingly,
women were a tiny minority. Thirty-three men spoke at the

Al-Azhar gathering but only three women, two of them from nearby institutions. Yet, I was warmly welcomed and graciously treated. Many faculty members and students in the audience expressed a strong interest in my presence there as a female educator and scholar. While most of those with whom I chatted were male, I can recall a particularly lively exchange with a cluster of young women from Malaysia who surrounded me after one of the formal sessions. Their questions ranged from the professional to the personal. They were as curious about my husband and children as about the books I had published. They are studying at Al-Azhar so that they can become religious leaders and teachers in their own country, and they form part of a fast-expanding vanguard of educated and inspiring young Muslims whose progress I will follow with eager enthusiasm.

A few concluding comments: (1) I have cited passages from the Qur'an by chapter (*sura* in Arabic) number and by verse number. For example, Q 24:35 refers to the twenty-fourth chapter of the Qur'an (traditionally entitled "The Light") and to the thirty-fifth verse within that chapter. Using these citations, readers can locate passages in the many different English translations that are currently available. While there can be slight variation in the verse numbering of some translations, context should be sufficient to avoid ambiguity. (2) Quotations from the Qur'an are from my *The Qur'an: A Norton Critical Edition* (New York, 2017). (3) Wherever possible I have avoided using Arabic terminology if a commonly found English translation exists or if the Arabic word finds frequent mention in popular publications. Examples of the latter would be terms like jihad or hijab. (4) Most importantly, I beg readers to bear in mind that demographers now reckon the world Muslim population to be 1.6 billion, and members of that population may be found in every country and culture on earth. Consequently, there is no single "Islam"; there is no single way of thinking and acting as a Muslim; and there is no single and unequivocal interpretation for any verse in the Qur'an. Recognizing that diversity, this book can offer succinct and straightforward responses to questions frequently asked about the Qur'an, but it cannot be—nor does it seek to be—the last word on the subject.

ACKNOWLEDGMENTS

This short book draws upon decades of teaching and research, decades during which I have been privileged to work with superb colleagues at several universities and colleges in both the United States and Canada, to interact with many more at conferences and invited lectures around the world, and to collaborate with a splendid cohort in producing the *Encyclopaedia of the Qur'an*. It is to this entire community of scholar-friends that I dedicate this book.

The question and answer format found here echoes exchanges that have animated my graduate and undergraduate classrooms and captures conversations that I have enjoyed with lecture audiences on this continent, in Britain and Europe, and in Egypt, Jordan, Lebanon, Turkey, Qatar, Saudi Arabia, the United Arab Emirates, Oman, India, Bangladesh, Malaysia, Indonesia, Japan, Korea, and China.

Many years of involvement with several forms of Muslim-Christian engagement have deepened my knowledge of both religious traditions. Participation in Roman Catholic interfaith efforts has been chiefly through the Pontifical Commission on Interreligious Dialogue and the Vatican's Commission for Religious Relations with Muslims. The Anglican Building Bridges Seminar, a long-standing effort begun by the Archbishop of Canterbury and now continued by Georgetown University, has offered the opportunity for sustained and productive dialogue with theologians both Muslim and Christian. A Muslim multinational enterprise launched in 2007 and entitled *A Common Word* has welcomed the cooperation of many non-Muslim scholars in its subsequent conferences and symposia.

Most especially, I would like to acknowledge the many Muslim students, colleagues, and friends who have become part of my life, both professionally and personally. I am grateful to professors in Cairo, Amman, and Damascus who corrected my Arabic, welcomed me into their homes, and often steered our conversations into matters of Islamic belief and practice. I am grateful to those whom I met at a university in Kuala Lumpur and a study center in Jakarta for providing a glimpse of life in the most populous part of the Muslim world. I am grateful to graduate students and research assistants who have refined my understanding of many aspects of the tradition that guides their lives. Finally, I am grateful to some wonderful educational institutions, Effat University in Saudi Arabia, Lady Shri Ram College for Women in India, the Asian University for Women in Bangladesh, Ewha Womens University in Korea, Tsuda University in Japan, and Nizwa University in Oman, for giving me opportunities to speak with, and to learn from, some of the brightest and most motivated students whom I have ever met.

The idea for this book began with Theo Calderara, a gifted and generous senior editor at Oxford University Press. I thank Theo for asking me to write this book, and I thank my Georgetown colleague, John Esposito, for encouraging me to accept the invitation.

PART I

THE BOOK AND WHY IT MATTERS

When you pull a copy of the Qur'an off a library shelf or pick one up in a bookshop, you'll find yourself holding a volume of average size and shape. You may spot an adjective in the title—"The Holy Qur'an" or "The Glorious Qur'an"—and flipping through the pages you may or may not see Arabic writing on one side and English on the other. You'll probably notice that there are different sections and that within the sections the text is further divided and numbered. If you turn to the first page and begin to read, some of the words will have a familiar ring, words like "God" and "Lord" and "merciful," and you'll soon realize that you're reading a prayer. Here it is in full:

1. In the name of God, the beneficent, the merciful.
2. Praise be to God, Lord of the worlds,
3. The beneficent, the merciful.
4. Owner of the day of judgment,
5. You (alone) do we worship; You (alone) do we ask for help.
6. Show us the straight path,
7. The path of those whom You have favored; not the (path) of those who earn Your anger nor of those who go astray.

But if you turn many more pages, that sense of familiarity will likely recede and questions will begin to crowd your mind: Where did this book come from? Who wrote it? What does its name mean? Who created this format for it and when was it put together? Why is it so important to millions—actually more than a billion and a half—people in this world? Our exploration of the Qur'an starts, then, with the historical context so that this scripture can be situated in its time and place. It begins with the Prophet Muhammad and the religious environment into which he was born and then explains how the Qur'an emerged during his lifetime and what happened in the decades after his death. From these basics the investigation can move to the shape and structure of the written text and to discussion of some of its literary characteristics and special passages. An understanding of how it is put together helps in addressing a frequently asked question: Why is the Qur'an so hard to read? People who have tried to tackle this text and found it difficult to do so can be forgiven for wondering how the Qur'an could matter so much to its believers. Delving into some key beliefs and practices will explain why the Qur'an is supremely important to Muslims and why its influence on both individuals and entire societies has been, and remains, so powerful. Knowing what Muslims, both Sunni and Shi'i, believe about the Qur'an and learning something about the care with which they treat the written text will help readers understand the place that it holds in Muslim minds and hearts.

1

ORIGINS

Where did the Qur'an come from?

Compared with other world scriptures—the Bible, the Bhagavad Gita, the Buddhist sutras, or the Dao De Jing—the Qur'an's history is reasonably clear and straightforward, at least as conveyed in traditional Muslim accounts. These accounts start, of course, with the Prophet Muhammad, who is described as a morally upright man and a spiritual seeker. Over a period of about two decades, these sources say, Muhammad received visions and heard voices that Muslims understand to be direct messages from God, via an angel identified as Gabriel. Muhammad proclaimed these divine revelations to his growing band of followers and eventually all the revelations were gathered together and organized into what we can now hold in our hands as the Qur'an. This traditional account situates these encounters between Muhammad and the angel in the Arabian Peninsula, specifically the western side of the peninsula that runs parallel to the Red Sea, in the towns of Mecca and Medina. The time frame is the early seventh century, roughly the same period that Buddhism was entering Tibet and that Irish monks were setting up monasteries in Scotland and the north of England.

But that is only part of the story. For Muslim believers, the Qur'an has an eternal prehistory. The real answer to "where did the Qur'an come from?" is simply that it came from God. It is important to emphasize that we are not talking about the divine inspiration of a human author. We are talking about God's direct speech. Muslims believe that the Qur'an, as it exists today, replicates exactly the divine words that were conveyed to Muhammad almost fourteen centuries ago.

Expanding upon many qur'anic verses that speak about God's "sending down" of the Qur'an, Muslim theologians have attempted to describe this descent, this process by which the Qur'an moved from God to its earthly recipient. Verse 85:21–22 speaks of "a glorious Qur'ān on a guarded tablet" and other verses refer to the "Mother of the Book." Both references have been taken to imply a heavenly archetype that is the ultimate source of all divine revelation, given first to earlier prophets like Moses and Jesus, and transmitted finally to Muhammad. As an intermediary stage, the Qur'an was sent down in its entirety to the lowest realm of heaven on the Night of Power (Q 97:1), and from there Gabriel brought sequential revelations to the Prophet Muhammad over the course of more than two decades. Commemorations of the Night of Power—and of the descent of the Qur'an—occur toward the end of Ramadan, the Muslim month of fasting.

Questions about the relation of the Qur'an, as God's speech, to God himself stimulated a major controversy in the first centuries of Islam. Was that speech a divine attribute—that is, was it eternal with God—or was it created by God? Eventually a majority consensus produced the Sunni doctrine of the Qur'an as eternal and uncreated, but not before much ink and blood had been spilled in defending both possibilities.

Who is Muhammad? Did he write the Qur'an?

Few men in history can claim the enduring impact achieved by Muhammad ibn 'Abdallah. He was born toward the end of the sixth century CE to a poor family in Mecca, a market town on the western side of the Arabian Peninsula. Orphaned early,

Muhammad found work with local trading caravans and as a young man attracted the attention of a wealthy widow who hired him and then married him. This marriage to Khadija bint Khuwaylid raised both his financial and social status, and Muhammad did not marry again until after her death.

In adulthood, he was known to withdraw to the outskirts of Mecca for periods of prayer and seclusion. During one such retreat, an angelic figure (later identified as Gabriel) appeared to Muhammad and proclaimed: "Recite: In the name of your Lord who created / Created man from a clot / Recite: And your Lord is the most bounteous / Who teaches by the pen / Teaches man what he knew not" (Q 96:1–5). The apparition startled Muhammad, who feared for his sanity and sought reassurance from his wife. Khadija managed to convince him that the revelation was divine, not demonic, and, along with a few others, she recognized him as a prophet of God. Among those whom she consulted was her cousin, a Christian monk named Waraqa. He, too, confirmed the authenticity of Muhammad's experience and declared him to be God's messenger.

Over the next two decades, these visionary incidents repeated themselves. Muhammad received the transmissions and, as his confidence in these experiences grew, began to tell his fellow Meccans about them, repeating verbatim what he had been told. Many of those who heard the messages, in turn, memorized them and passed them on to others. The core message that Muhammad preached to them identified God (*Allah* in Arabic) as the creator of all, the creator who has generously given humans all that they need to flourish and to whom humans owe exclusive worship and unending gratitude. Just as God has been just and generous to humans, they must be equally just and generous to each other. Muhammad's early preaching carried strong denunciations of the Meccan elite for their abuse of the poor and the unprotected. Of course, these elites resented such criticism and rejected Muhammad's efforts to foster social and religious reform, finally forcing him to flee the city to protect himself and his growing band of followers.

The Prophet immigrated to a city about two hundred miles north of Mecca and quickly assumed both political and religious leadership of his new home, Medina. This emigration in 622 CE was a watershed event for the new community and marks year one of the Muslim calendar. After repeated hostilities between his followers in Medina and the people of Mecca, Muhammad's community triumphed and made a victorious return to his birthplace and to its central shrine, the Ka'ba. During this entire period, Muhammad continued to receive revelations, all of which were eventually collected and assembled into the Qur'an. After a final pilgrimage (*hajj* in Arabic) to the Ka'ba, Muhammad died in 632 and was buried in Medina.

Muslims believe that while God sent many prophets before Muhammad—including Abraham, Moses, and Jesus—he is the last one, the "seal of the prophets." Over the following centuries, many would succeed Muhammad as religious and political leaders of the Muslim community, but none of them would be ranked as prophets. Muslim belief also holds that Muhammad was illiterate (*ummi* in Arabic). Consequently, he could not have written the Qur'an; it comes directly from God. God revealed this scripture to Muhammad just as he had revealed earlier scriptures to Moses, Jesus, and others, and he revealed it in Arabic.

While Muhammad and Jesus are often compared as the founding figures of what have become the world's two largest religions, the difference in beliefs about them is important. Christians deify Jesus; for them, he is God as a human, a human who was born, lived, died and—crucially—was resurrected from the dead. Muslims do not believe that Muhammad is God, or that he is a manifestation of the divine. Muhammad is a human being, albeit a holy, sinless, and venerated human being. Among Muslims, devotion to the Prophet Muhammad runs deep, and the imitation of his exemplary life and virtuous qualities shapes daily practice. Muslims revere him as the perfect model and as a source of divine grace and benefaction. The multiple roles that the Prophet embodied during his lifetime have directed the development of Islamic thought. Political philosophers see Muhammad as the perfect ruler, commander, and statesman. Mystics revere him for charting the course to spiritual enlightenment. Jurists draw upon his decisions and pronouncements to shape the structures of Islamic law.

Especially after World War II, as postcolonial reform movements transformed the Muslim world, reformist ideologies looked to Muhammad's leadership in Medina as proof that the religious and the political are inextricably intertwined. The sociopolitical significance of his example validated Islam as a complete and comprehensive system of life, a robust alternative to Western models, and one that is fully compatible with modernity in all its aspects.

Why does the Qur'an carry that name?

First, let's deal with the different English spellings of this word. "Koran" was an early attempt to mimic the pronunciation of the Arabic term, but that transcription has been largely replaced with the more accurate "Qur'an" (or Quran). Most major newspapers and other print media have now switched to this rendering, but it is still worth using both spellings when doing a library or an online search.

The verb that underlies the classical Arabic word *qur'ān* signifies "collecting" and "drawing together." By extension, the term carries the sense of "reading" or "recitation," since it is the collecting and joining together of words that create meanings to be recited or read. Another combination of the same Arabic letters gives us the imperative verb *iqra'*, usually translated as "recite," the command to Muhammad when he begins receiving divine messages. The emphasis on recitation pervades the Qur'an since revelation happens not as a silent, interior experience, but as a series of discrete oral discourses transmitted from God through an angelic intermediary to the Prophet Muhammad.

The Qur'an associates itself with previous revelations, most explicitly in Q 9:111: "God has bought from the believers their lives and their wealth because the garden will be theirs: they shall fight in the way of God and shall slay and be slain. It is a promise which is binding on Him in the Torah and the Gospel and the Qur'ān." In this verse the term "Qur'ān" comes closer to a sense of the full collection of divine disclosures, a complete "scripture" like the earlier Hebrew Bible and New Testament.

In addition to being called "The Recitation," other names for the Qur'an have been drawn from verses throughout the text. The most prominent of these names is "The Book," as in Q 29:51: "Is it not enough for them that We have sent down to you (Muhammad) the Book which is read to them?" Sometimes "The Book" has a wider meaning and includes the earlier Jewish and Christian scriptures, what the Qur'an calls the Torah and the Gospel. In similar fashion, the Qur'an claims a primordial connection to "the Mother of the Book," the record of all events, past, present, and future, and the source of all scriptures. According to Q 43:4, this celestial archetype resides with God: "And in the Mother of the Book, which We possess, it is indeed sublime, decisive."

Among other names for the Qur'an are "The Remembrance," "The Light," "The Wisdom," and "The Criterion." Nowadays, Muslims generally refer to the Qur'an as "the Holy Qur'an," or "the Noble Qur'an," or "the Glorious Qur'an," and many English translations carry one of these titles.

How long did it take to finish the Qur'an?

Here is the most important fact about the timeline of the Qur'an: the present arrangement of the text does not match the sequence of its revelation. While Muslims assert that an archetypal form of all divine revelation, the Mother of the Book, has existed from all eternity, they understand the earthly Qur'an to be a discrete set of revelations that was delivered, disseminated, collected, and compiled in the first half of the seventh century. It is a text that came together in the full light of history and within a defined period of time. Historians of ancient Arabic literature situate the Qur'an at the culminating point of the early, oral—and primarily poetical—tradition.

According to traditional Muslim accounts, God presented his revelation to the Prophet Muhammad in segments, not as one continuous transmission. The total time span of this sequence is usually counted as about twenty-three years. But in classical Islamic thought, this period follows the "descent" of the entire Qur'an to a heavenly realm on the Night of Power (Q 97:1–5), an event commemorated during the fasting month of Ramadan.

Q 96:1–5, the passage that begins, "Recite: In the name of your Lord," has usually been reckoned as the first part of the Qur'an, and the story of its proclamation has been described in the previous section on Muhammad. Clearly it does not appear as the Qur'an's first chapter (sura in Arabic), but is found close to the end of the 114 suras. Scholars have also debated which was the final message given to Muhammad. Two verses dominate these debates, both of which carry a concluding tone: "And guard yourselves against a day in which you will be brought back to God. Then every soul will be paid in full what it has earned, and they will not be wronged" (Q 2:281); and "This day have I perfected your religion for you and completed My favor to you, and have chosen for you as religion al-Islam" (Q 5:3).

Since the order of passages in the Qur'an does not match the sequence in which they were revealed, we can ask whether attempts have been made to reconstruct that sequence. Actually, a great deal of effort has been expended by Muslim and non-Muslim scholars to create such reconstructions. Most of these place the primary division between what Muhammad received when he lived in Mecca (610–622 CE) and what was revealed to him after he had moved to Medina (622–632 CE). Printed copies of the Qur'an note this basic division in the headings of individual chapters. While medieval scholarly literature reflects some disagreements, consensus eventually formed around a list that marked eighty-six chapters as Meccan and twenty-eight as Medinan.

Beyond the Meccan/Medinan divide, further specification relied upon evidence from the Qur'an itself, as well as from external sources. These analyses were not prompted simply by historical curiosity; the results could have legal implications. Depending upon the chronological ordering of verses, a later revelation could be taken to nullify or abrogate an earlier one. Lists of such "abrogating" and "abrogated" verses became a staple of Muslim scholarship on the Qur'an. Pursued from another angle, sources such as the Prophet's biography and accounts of his military campaigns were studied for any insight they could shed on particular revelations. This, too, generated a subfield of qur'anic studies known as "the occasions of revelation."

The topic of the Qur'an's chronology attracted considerable attention from Western scholars, beginning in the nineteenth century. A succession of German works refined the Meccan/Medinan categorization with further subdivisions. While that analysis has been widely accepted, more recent work on the interpolation of material from one period into suras classified as dating to another has raised questions about the very possibility of determining a precise chronological order of the Qur'an's suras. Very detailed literary analysis of qur'anic elements, such as form, style, and rhyme, are also increasing our understanding of the structural history of the text.

Did Muhammad know anything about other religions?

The Arabian Peninsula in the centuries before Muhammad could be called—to use a contemporary term—a "multireligious environment." While there has been less archaeological investigation in Arabia than in other parts of the Middle East, material evidence of shrines and sanctuaries has been unearthed, and inscriptions, particularly from South Arabia, have been intensively studied. The Qur'an and other early Islamic texts portray the native Arabs of that era as devoted to various deities—including a "high god" known as Allah—many of whom were housed and honored in the central shrine of Mecca, the Ka'ba. Muslim belief credits the prophet Abraham and his son Ishmael with building this cube-shaped shrine that became a pilgrimage site for tribes from all over the Arabian Peninsula and a source of income for the leaders of Mecca.

While tribal gods were venerated, they did not control individual destinies. The larger, impersonal force of fate or time governed the span of one's life and its major events. Nor was human behavior subject to the judgment of these gods; rather, tribal values of honor, valor, kinship loyalty, and hospitality created standards of morality and ethics.

Jewish and Christian communities of various types dotted the Arabian Peninsula. The biographies of Muhammad attest to the presence of Christians in Mecca, and Medina was home to some large Jewish tribes. Christian tribal confederations on the northern borders of the peninsula aligned themselves with the neighboring Byzantine and Persian empires. Najran, an oasis town in the southern part of the peninsula, became the site of an early Christian community, as did the tribal confederation of Kinda in central Arabia. Islamic tradition speaks of a delegation of Christians from Najran who visited Muhammad in Mecca, and a passage in the Qur'an (Q 3:61–62) has been understood to reflect a proposed disputation between Muslims and Christians about the true identity of Jesus. Many references in the Qur'an, both direct and indirect, argue for the prevalence of Christians and Christian ideas in seventh-century Arabia.

While there is textual evidence that Jews resided in various parts of the Arabian Peninsula, we know most about those groups that lived in or near Medina. Biographies of the Prophet Muhammad describe an initially amicable, but later more contentious, relationship between the newly arrived Muslim emigrants and the established Jewish tribes of this city. As with Christianity, many verses in the Qur'an reveal an awareness of Jewish beliefs and practices, some of which are lauded and others condemned. The Qur'an addresses the Jews as "Children of Israel," and they, along with the Christians, are included in the qur'anic category of the "People of the Book." In some respects, they are recognized as believers, while in others they are rejected as unbelievers. Disappointment in the Jewish rejection of Muhammad's claim to be a prophet could be read as a theme across the Qur'an. Because they, too, attested strongly to the oneness of God, Muhammad and his followers expected the Jews of Medina to embrace this new prophet and were startled and angered by their refusal to do so.

Within the last few decades, a wave of research has expanded the boundaries of earlier work on qur'anic origins. The study of Late Antiquity, promoted chiefly by scholars of Roman and Byzantine history, has drawn upon other languages and literatures, such as Coptic, Aramaic, Middle Persian, and, especially, Syriac. Related work on Christian communities in Ethiopia and on the contested category of Jewish Christians raises questions about the kinds of Jewish and Christian doctrine that find reference and rebuttal in the Qur'an.

What happened to the Qur'an after Muhammad died?

Muslim history and tradition carry time-honored accounts of how the Qur'an went from being a years-long series of discrete revelations to a written and invariant text. Although these accounts differ in some of their particulars, the main points can be quickly summarized: some sections of the Qur'an may have achieved written form during the Prophet's lifetime, but most of it was carried in the minds and memories of his followers. As individuals in this early group became casualties of wars and raids, concerns that parts of God's revelation would be irretrievably lost led the first caliph, Abu Bakr (r. 632–634), to commission a "collection" of everything that could be culled from written fragments and human memory. When Abu Bakr died, this *mushaf*—the Arabic name for a written text of the Qur'an—was given to Hafsa, a widow of Muhammad and a daughter of the second caliph, Umar (r. 634–644).

Other, similar efforts resulted in the proliferation of such collections and concerns about their competing authority. To solve this dilemma, the third caliph, 'Uthman (r. 644–656), ordered the destruction of these rival efforts and the creation of a definitive version based on Abu Bakr's collection. This was then disseminated as the authoritative assemblage, and Muslim belief enshrines this " 'Uthmanic *mushaf*" as the complete record of God's revelations to Muhammad. Its chapters (suras) were organized and ordered into the final form in which the text still exists today.

While complete in most respects, the 'Uthmanic compilation remained vulnerable to variation. At that early stage in the development of Arabic writing, the script functioned as something of a shorthand, lacking reliable ways of marking vowels and certain consonants. Consequently, the same skeletal script could be pronounced in various ways. While some of these different readings were inconsequential, others were not. For example, Shi'is read certain verses (e.g., Q 75:17 and 35:56) as supporting their claims for the primacy of 'Ali ibn Abi Talib (d. 661), the Prophet's son-in-law and the fourth caliph, and of 'Ali's lineage. Eventually, the text was given full markings and vocalization, an effort ordinarily attributed to a tenth-century linguist from Baghdad, Abu Bakr Ahmad ibn Mujahid (d. ca. 935). Ibn Mujahid stabilized the consonantal structure of the Qur'an and restricted the range of valid vocalizations to seven. While some additional variety was eventually accepted, it should be emphasized that the significance of these variations was not great. In modern times, one of these vocalizations has gained predominance in the Muslim world (codified by a scholarly commission in Cairo in 1920s) and can be found in most printed texts of the Arabic Qur'an.

Non-Muslim scholarship has questioned the reliability of this Muslim history for generations and has done so with increased attention in the last several decades. In 1999, the *Atlantic Monthly* brought such debates to a popular audience with an article that laid out controversial new theories and described manuscript discoveries, like those in the Great Mosque of Sana'a, Yemen, which raised questions about beliefs in the invariant nature of the qur'anic text. More recently, the *New York Times* has played to public interest in these issues with articles about ancient Qur'an fragments discovered at the University of Birmingham and the University of Tübingen. Carbon-dating analysis by labs in Oxford and Zurich, respectively, offer a high probability that both finds date from the seventh century, thus providing documentary evidence in support of traditional Muslim textual history and arguing against some of the more radical revisionist claims.

2

STRUCTURE

Does the Qur'an have different parts?

Compared to the Bible or the library of Buddhist scriptures, the Qur'an is not a very long book. While the Bible is an assemblage of many books whose composition coalesced over more than a millennium, the Qur'an is a single book proclaimed over a period of about twenty-three years. The Prophet Muhammad received those revelations, according to traditional Muslim belief, as oral communications from the angel Gabriel. He, in turn, preached them to the expanding group of disciples who were drawn to his religious vision. Many memorized what they heard, while others may have preserved some parts in writing. After Muhammad's death, a series of efforts to assemble and organize these divine revelations resulted, eventually, in a fixed corpus. In its final form, the Qur'an has been passed down in both oral and written form from one generation to the next. Muslims believe that the Qur'an they memorize and read today contains God's own words, as faithfully transmitted from the time of their first revelation.

Just as the Bible is divided into books and verses, the Qur'an is divided into textual units that are usually called chapters in English (*suras* in Arabic) and into verses (*ayat* in Arabic). There are 114 suras in all, of widely varying lengths. Some are as short as just a few verses, while the longest, the second sura, runs to 286 ayat. Each sura has a name, usually a distinctive word drawn from some part of the sura, and Muslims ordinarily cite passages in the Qur'an by sura name and verse number. Examples of these names are "the Cow" (sura 2), "the Angels" (sura 35), "the Pen" (sura 68), and "the Disbelievers" (sura 109). Each sura but one is preceded by the invocation known as the *basmala*, "In the name of God, the Beneficent, the Merciful."

As previously noted, the arrangement of suras in the Qur'an as a written text does not match the order in which they were revealed to Muhammad. Apart from the short first sura, known as "the Opening," the ordering principle is, for the most part, that of decreasing length. With some exceptions, the longest suras are positioned at the beginning of the text and the shortest toward the end. A similar structuring has been found in a few other scriptures, with some scholars pointing to the roughly descending size of the Epistles of Paul in the New Testament as an example. Yet, neither Muslim nor Western scholars have provided a compelling explanation for this arrangement.

Muslim scholars have been studying and discussing the Qur'an for centuries, trying to figure out which verses came to Muhammad in the early years of his preaching and which came later. Medieval scholars, using both internal and external criteria, achieved consensus on a division of suras that assigned some to the Meccan period (610–622) of the Prophet's ministry and some to his Medinan years (622–632). Viewed very generally, the earlier Meccan suras urgently exhort worship of the one God, predict the coming Day of Judgment, point to the stunning testimony of God's creation, and depict the divine wrath visited upon earlier peoples who rejected their prophets. The later Medinan suras reflect a different context. Muhammad and his followers controlled the political, social, and military structures of the city and its region, so the revelations reflect the issues and concerns that building and guiding such a community entails.

In 1967 a Sudanese intellectual published a slim volume entitled *The Second Message of Islam*. The thesis proposed by Mahmud Muhammad Taha (d. 1985) in this book upends much Islamic legal reasoning by making the division between Meccan and Medinan verses the basis for a new vision of Islam. Taha relegates Medinan material to the past, noting that it was important for the nascent Muslim community of seventh-century Arabia but is outmoded and irrelevant today. True Islam, the enduring divine vision that supports human dignity, equality of the sexes, and religious freedom, may be found in the Meccan verses. Taha was executed for apostasy in 1985, but his influence has continued to grow. A *New Yorker* profile in 2006 dubbed him "the moderate martyr" and the 1996 English translation of his book accelerated its circulation among progressive Muslims.

Today's printed copies of the Qur'an identify suras as Meccan or Medinan in a prefatory heading. Western post-Enlightenment research has suggested a further division of the Meccan period into three sub-periods, a hypothesis that has received broad support among European and American scholars of the Qur'an, but less acceptance among Muslim scholars. In addition to this Meccan/Medinan identification, copies of the Qur'an carry marginal markings that represent ways of dividing the text for devotional or liturgical purposes. Some marks divide the text into seven parts to facilitate the reading or recitation of the Qur'an over the course of a week. Other marks indicate a division into thirty parts, one for each day of the month. These demarcations support the popular practice of the daily reading or reciting of a set portion of the Qur'an during the fasting month of Ramadan.

Divisions of the Qur'an, whether determined by geography (Mecca and Medina) or by textual lengths (seven parts, thirty parts, etc.), play an important role in qur'anic scholarship and in the ritual use of the Qur'an. They shape the formal structure of the Qur'an in both its printed and its manuscript copies. Structural studies at the level of the sura, however, represent another mode of qur'anic investigation. Some modern commentators, both Muslim and non-Muslim, have focused attention on the textual unity of individual suras—especially the longer suras—seeking to uncover rhetorical patterns and central themes. Methodologies used for other literature, such as the Homeric epics and the Hebrew Bible, have been applied to the Qur'an, but the results have not always won acceptance from other scholars.

Why do people say that the Qur'an is hard to read?

Frequently, friends and colleagues, as well as those whom I teach and those to whom I lecture about the Qur'an, ask me a simple, straightforward question: "Why is it so hard to read the Qur'an?" These questioners have often picked up an English translation of the Qur'an. They open it to the first chapter (sura) and set themselves the task of reading straight through. Before too long, they find themselves in sympathy with the noted Victorian philosopher and essayist, Thomas Carlyle (d. 1881), who complained that the Qur'an "is as toilsome reading as I ever undertook. A wearisome confused jumble, crude, incondite; endless iterations, long-windedness, entanglement. [. . .] Nothing but a sense of duty could carry any European through the Koran."

Other judgments have been less harsh. The illustrious German poet J. W. Goethe (d. 1832) found fault but also felt attraction: "The style of the Koran, in accordance with its contents and aim is stern, grand, terrible, here and there truly sublime." Even more laudatory is the oft-cited description of Marmaduke Pickthall (d. 1936), the twentieth-century British convert to Islam and translator of the Qur'an, who characterized the Qur'an as an "inimitable symphony, the very sounds of which move men to tears and ecstasy."

Nevertheless, many first-time readers lodge a litany of complaints. The text jumps from one topic to another. The genres are jumbled—prayers, oaths, cautionary words, lyric descriptions of Paradise can all occur within a short section. The voice or speaker moves from the first to the third to the second person without warning. There are no "stories"—that is, there are few extended narratives with developed plot lines. Usually such readers come to the Qur'an with a notion of "scripture" shaped by the Bible. They expect a text that is similarly organized, one with a linear forward-facing chronology. Much scholarly effort, both Muslim and non-Muslim, has been expended trying to explain the structure and stylistic elements of the Qur'an, with Muslim commentators finding theological justifications and non-Muslim academics seeking insights from other pieces of Semitic literature.

Perhaps Pickthall's reference to "sounds" starts to solve the conundrum. The Qur'an is a recitation before it is a reading. In the mouth of a skilled reciter, the language comes alive and captures hearts as much as minds. Remember that most Muslims in most centuries—like most people everywhere—were illiterate. They did not read the Qur'an; they heard it recited and often learned and memorized portions to recite themselves. Another clue is chronology. According to Muslim belief, many of the first suras that Muhammad received are toward the end of the book. Young Muslims usually start with those when they are learning the Qur'an, and many American professors in university classes on Islam urge their students to do likewise. The vivid images and urgent exhortations of these passages can orient the novice reader to the Qur'an's extraordinary impact on its original audience.

Are some parts of the Qur'an more important than others?

In one sense, the answer to this question is "no." Since the entire Qur'an is understood to be divine speech, gradations of value and importance cannot apply. Nevertheless, some parts of the Qur'an have achieved special prominence because of their association with life-cycle events, with religious worship, and with special blessings. For example, observant Muslims recite the first sura, a short passage called "The Opening," several times a day as part of the fivefold prayer cycle: "In the name of God, the beneficent, the merciful / Praise be to God, Lord of the worlds / The beneficent, the merciful / Owner of the day of judgment / You (alone) do we worship; You (alone) do we ask for help / Show us the straight path / The path of those whom You have favored; not the (path) of those who earn Your anger nor of those who go astray" (Q 1:1–7). These seven verses, frequently compared to the Christian "Lord's Prayer," capture essential themes of Muslim belief.

This sura begins, as does every sura but one in the Qur'an, with the short invocation known in Arabic as the *basmala*. That word comes from the phrase itself, "In the name of God, the beneficent, the merciful" (*bi-smi llahi l-rahmani l-rahim*). Muslims around the world, whatever their native tongues, repeat this phrase frequently, especially when beginning an action of consequence, such as a speech, a meal, or an exam. On the airlines of some Muslim countries a recorded voice will intone the basmala as the plane is taxiing for takeoff. Although its status as an actual verse of the Qur'an is debated, many believe that the basmala carries special blessings which account for its common use in amulets and other talismans. Elaborate calligraphic representations of this invocation have made it an object of Islamic art, both medieval and modern.

Another significant verse that stresses the oneness and omnipotence of God is Q 2:255. Like a handful of qur'anic verses, it acquired a special title, the "Throne Verse," a name drawn from its declaration that God's "throne includes the heavens and the earth, and He is never weary of preserving them." The "Verse of Piety," Q 2:177, provides a succinct catalogue of Muslim belief and practice:

> It is not righteousness that you turn your faces to the east and the west; but righteous is he who believes in God and the last day and the angels and the scripture

and the prophets; and gives his wealth, for love of Him, to kin and to orphans and the needy and the wayfarer and to those who ask, and to set slaves free; and observes proper worship and pays the poor-tax. And those who keep their treaty when they make one, and the patient in tribulation and adversity and time of stress. Such are they who are sincere. Such are the God-fearing.

Other named verses include the "Light Verse" (Q 24:35) and the "Sword Verse" (Q 9:5), as well as such special suras as Q 36 (*Surat Yasin*) and Q 112 (*Surat al-Ikhlas*).

The particular qualities accorded certain verses became enshrined in a genre of Islamic religious literature known as "the virtues/merits of the Qur'an." These works not only laud the study and recitation of the Qur'an as a whole, but also detail the designated spiritual blessings and rewards that accrue to certain verses and suras, such as those just discussed.

Is the Qur'an poetry or prose or both?

Muslim scholars, both ancient and modern, are adamant in their assertions that the Qur'an is not poetry. In several passages, the Qur'an itself insists that Muhammad is not a poet. Why would this be an issue? What's behind such determined denials? The answers to that are both historical and literary. Poetry has an ancient place in Arab culture, and poets, at least some poets, were revered figures in their clans and tribes. Their ability to evoke Bedouin ideals and to praise famous kinsmen in rich, rhythmic language won them renown and patronage. Even today, Arabs relish the memorization and recitation of their classical poetry.

While poetry could praise, it could also mock, mimic, and curse. In the world of ancient Arabia, many believed that poets were possessed, that they could perform magic, that unnatural or demonic forces prompted their prophecies and soothsaying. By his adversaries, Muhammad was charged with being a poet, a person possessed, and qur'anic passages record these charges and issue decisive denials. For example, Q 21:5 exclaims, "'No,' they say [of Muhammad's preaching], '(these are but) muddled dreams; no, he has only invented it; no, he is but a poet. Let him bring us a sign even as those of old (who were God's messengers) were sent (with signs)'." A version of this involves accusations of madness, as with Q 15:6, "And they say: 'O you to whom the reminder [the Qur'an] is revealed, you are indeed a madman!'" and Q 37:36, "And said: 'shall we forsake our gods for a mad poet?'." The Arabic word here translated as "mad" literally means possessed by jinn, the supernatural beings who can take different shapes and forms, including human.

Despite the qur'anic abhorrence of poetry and its practitioners, poets continued to exert strong cultural influence in Arabic-speaking lands and in those regions conquered and colonized by Muslim warriors. By the tenth and eleventh centuries, Muslim mystics (i.e., Sufis) composed devotional lyrics to express their spiritual longings, often using the imagery of human love as a metaphor for union with the divine. In later centuries, revered Sufi saints became the subject of praise poems that remain popular to this day. The most famous praise poems, however, are those recited to honor the Prophet Muhammad on the annual commemoration of his birthday. This celebration, which falls during the third month of the Islamic calendar, is often a national holiday in Muslim countries and a time of great festivities. Public proclamation of poems that pay homage to Muhammad and recount the events of his life are often interspersed with the recitation of verses from the Qur'an.

3

BELIEFS ABOUT

Why do Muslims say that the Qur'an is God's own word?

First of all, Muslims mean that the Qur'an is not Muhammad's speech and was not written by him; it does not record divinely inspired images and ideas that he formulated and then presented in his own words. Muslims firmly believe that the Arabic words, phrases, and sentences of the Qur'an come directly from God. They were conveyed to the Prophet through the angel Gabriel. Put succinctly, this is a doctrine of divine dictation, not divine inspiration. Here is how the historical sources explain the process: the Prophet Muhammad, who was known for his periods of spiritual withdrawal, began to experience vivid dreams and other premonitions. Suddenly and unexpectedly, the angel Gabriel appeared to him and ordered the Prophet to "Recite." Muhammad was confused so Gabriel repeated the command, finally telling the Prophet the divine words that he was to repeat and remember. This scenario, depicted in Q 96 and elaborated in later sources, began the twenty-year span of the Qur'an's revelation. The process was both visual and auditory. Muhammad could see the angel Gabriel and could hear the divine words that he transmitted.

Receiving this divine dictation was not an easy or painless experience for the Prophet. Many stories describe the physical side effects, everything from the sound of bells ringing, to intense sweating and fainting, to the sensation of being pressed down with a heavy weight.

There are spatial and temporal dimensions to the transmission of God's word. The Qur'an "comes down" or "is sent down." The direction is one way, from the celestial realm to the world below, and the initiative is always God's. God has "sent down" the same message to previous prophets and messengers: "We inspire you [Muḥammad] as We inspired Noah and the prophets after him, as We inspired Abraham and Ishmael and Isaac and Jacob and the tribes, and Jesus and Job and Jonah and Aaron and Solomon, and as we imparted to David the Psalms" (Q 4:163).

Recognizing this, in many passages the Qur'an characterizes itself as "confirming" previous revelations. All are God's word, and the Qur'an is God's final word. In later Islamic theology the spatial and temporal dimensions of divine revelation come together in the doctrine of a heavenly book, an eternal archetype from which all revelation proceeds. The concept of "God's word" is used in another sense beside that of divine revelation. It is God's creative command: "The originator of the heavens and the earth! When He decrees a thing, He says to it only: 'Be!' and it is" (Q 2:117).

Who is Gabriel and what is his connection to the Qur'an?

The angel Gabriel, called *Jibril* in Arabic, was the principal conduit of the Qur'an's revelation to the Prophet Muhammad. Generally, Muslims do not believe that God communicated with Muhammad directly but rather that he used Gabriel as his messenger. Although Gabriel is mentioned by name only three times in the Qur'an, his first mention makes his role clear: "Say (O Muḥammad, to mankind): 'Who is an enemy to Gabriel! For he it is who has revealed (this scripture) to your heart by God's permission, confirming what was (revealed) before it, and a guidance and glad tidings to believers'" (Q 2:97).

Later Islamic literature, particularly the hadith (a record of Muhammad's words and actions) and the Prophet's biography, offer detailed accounts of Muhammad's multiple encounters with this angelic being. When Gabriel confronted the Prophet with the command to "Recite!" Muhammad was confounded, not knowing what to do or how to respond. After being pressed repeatedly by this stranger to "Recite! In the name of your Lord" (Q 96:1–2), Muhammad sought consolation from his wife. She reassured him that he had not been the subject of a satanic attack and consulted her elderly Christian cousin, who confirmed that her husband had been visited by God's angel of revelation.

Although he is not named, commentators on the Qur'an regularly identify Gabriel with the person who appears to the Prophet in the visionary sequence depicted in Q 53:1–18. Here Muhammad encountered "one of mighty powers" who "grew clear to view" and then "drew near" until he was "two bows' length or even nearer, and he revealed to His servant what he revealed."

Gabriel also figures in the Qur'an's account of the annunciation to Mary, the mother of Jesus, that she would bear a child:

And make mention of Mary in the scripture, when
    she had withdrawn from her people to a chamber
    looking east,
And had chosen seclusion from them. Then We sent to
    her Our spirit and it assumed for her the likeness of a
    perfect man.
She said: "I seek refuge in the Beneficent one from you,
    if you are God-fearing."
He said: "I am only a messenger of your Lord, that
    I may bestow on you a faultless son."
She said: "How can I have a son when no mortal has
    touched me, neither have I been unchaste?"
He said: "So (it will be). Your Lord says: 'It is easy for
    Me. And (it will be) that We may make of him a

revelation for mankind and a mercy from Us, and it is a thing ordained.'" (Q 19:16–21)

Given Gabriel's centrality to the act of revelation and his multiple appearances in the Qur'an, it is not surprising that later Islamic philosophical, theological, and mystical literature elaborates on this figure and his cosmological and spiritual roles.

Does the Qur'an talk about itself?

Even the casual reader of the Qur'an will quickly encounter phrases like "It is a glorious Qur'an on a preserved tablet" (Q 85:21–22); "We, even We, have revealed to you the Qur'ān, a revelation" (Q 76:23); "And this Qur'ān is not such as could ever be invented except by God" (Q 10:38); "We narrate to you (Muḥammad) the best of narratives in that We have inspired in you this Qur'ān, though before you were of the heedless" (Q 12:3); "When before it there was the scripture of Moses, an example and a mercy; and this is a confirming scripture in the Arabic language, that it may warn those who do wrong and bring good tidings for the righteous" (Q 46:12). Or perhaps most directly, the earliest such declaration in the text: "This is the scripture of which there is no doubt, a guidance to those who ward off (evil)" (Q 2:2). In a fashion far different from the Bible, the Qur'an frequently refers to itself. This self-referential or self-reflexive quality of the Qur'an distinguishes it from earlier scriptures and points to the context of its origin.

A variable vocabulary—book, remembrance, glad tidings, warning, sending down, parable, wisdom, guidance, clear message—defines and designates the Qur'an and allows it to mark different facets of its message. While the Qur'an frequently states and underscores what it *is*, it also makes clear what it is *not*: it is not, for example, "a lie that he [Muḥammad] has invented . . . fables of the men of old which he has had written down" (Q 25:4–5). One of the infrequent instances of

self-referentiality in the New Testament provides an intima-
tion of this: "It was not on tales artfully spun that we relied,
when we told you of the power of our Lord Jesus Christ and
his coming" (2 Peter 1:16).

The Qur'an entered an environment already suffused with
notions of sacred books. Echoes of previous scriptures and of
a common core of what has been dubbed "monotheistic folklore" can be found throughout the text. Given this context,
competing claims to divine authority were inevitable. Are these
qur'anic self-descriptions a "strategy of self-authorization," as
some have claimed? The repeated assurances of the Qur'an's
divine origin, of its unassailable veracity, of its confirmation
and correction of all previous revelations certainly suggest an
arena of inter-religious polemic and argumentation. One can
hear in such qur'anic assertions the response to challenges,
the direct counter to charges that Muhammad is not a true
prophet, that the words he conveys are nothing but his own
misguided musings.

Do Muslims believe that the Qur'an existed from all eternity?

The essential debate goes like this: If God is eternal and the
Qur'an is God's speech, then the Qur'an must be eternal.
That, in fact, became the dominant, orthodox position—but
not without generating significant controversy and even conflict. In the minds of many, to say that the Qur'an is eternal
cuts dangerously close to asserting that there is something that
exists alongside God, something that has a status akin to his.
How can that assertion be reconciled with the core qur'anic
idea that God is totally other, that "there is none like him" (Q
42:11)?

The debate heated up in the eighth century when early
Muslim scholars began to ask, "What does it mean to talk
about 'God's speech' or about 'the word of God'?" Clearly,
God's speech is not like that of humans, so how does it
occur? In trying to bridge the conceptual gap between God

as essentially other and speech as an event in time and space, these thinkers interpreted various qur'anic phrases—"the Mother of the Book (Q 13:35, 43:4, 3:7), the "Hidden Book" (Q 56:78), and the "Preserved Tablet" (Q 85:22), to mean a primordial holy book.

This heavenly prototype sits in God's presence and is the foundation of the Qur'an, of all previous scriptures, and of all God's decrees. God drew his revelations to the Prophet from this source. The final days of Ramadan commemorate the Night of Power when the whole Qur'an was sent from the heavenly book to the lowest heaven. From there Gabriel conveyed it at intervals to Muhammad over twenty-some years.

The concept of the "Preserved Tablet" did not really solve the matter, however, because the question of whether that, too, was created or co-eternal with God immediately arose. Nor did the debate remain a simple scholarly exchange. It became contentious and political. In 833 the seventh Abbasid caliph, al-Ma'mun (r. 809–833) ordered all the leading scholars to proclaim their belief in the createdness of the Qur'an. Refusal to do so could result in the confiscation of property, imprisonment, and torture, or even in death. In his proclamation of this order, al-Ma'mun likened the Muslim belief in an uncreated Qur'an to the Christian belief in an uncreated word of God (i.e., Jesus).

What has been dubbed the Islamic "inquisition" lasted for more than two decades, principally in Baghdad but also in other provinces of the ninth-century Islamic empire. Although various explanations have been offered for this purge, the most obvious reason would be an unambiguous assertion of the caliph's power: the final say in all matters, including doctrinal matters, belongs to the caliph, not to religious scholars. Although the "inquisition" eventually dissipated, it fortified the dogma of the uncreated or eternal Qur'an as a permanent feature of Islamic teaching.

Are all Qur'ans exactly the same or do different Muslim groups have different Qur'ans?

During the twelve-year reign of the third caliph, 'Uthman (r. 644–656), the revelations that Muhammad had received throughout the final decades of his life achieved the form and format that exist today. The completed Qur'an comprised 114 chapters (suras) arranged in their present sequence. The Arabic text, however, was written without all the eventual vowel signs, diacritical points, and markers to show the end of verses and of suras. Given the peculiarities of Arabic writing, this created ambiguity in the understanding of some words and phrases in the Qur'an until the early tenth century when a fully voweled text was established.

According to standard accounts, when this 'Uthmanic standard text or canonical text was promulgated, other existing codices of the Qur'an were collected and destroyed. Nevertheless, classical Qur'anic literature mentions manuscripts that may have escaped this destruction and makes note of some textual variants.

A significant dispute between Sunni and Shi'i Islam revolves around the integrity of this 'Uthmanic codex. Particularly in the first centuries of Islam, Shi'is argued that the text had been falsified through the deliberate omission of certain words and phrases and the equally deliberate addition of others. Some traditions even quantify these charges, enumerating how many words were omitted and how many were added. According to many early Shi'is, the true Qur'an would have mentioned 'Ali ibn Abi Talib, the Prophet's cousin and son-in-law. 'Ali was also the fourth caliph and a crucial link in the claim that leadership of the Muslim community rightly resides in Muhammad's bloodline.

By the tenth century, with the ascendency of Shi'i political and dynastic fortunes, these accusations subsided. Charges of actual falsification receded, although the notion that parts of the Qur'an had been lost remained a feature of Shi'i thought.

While contemporary Sunnis and Shi'is read, recite, and pray from the same Qur'an, they may own copies with different introductions and annotations. Such addenda may present the Shi'i interpretation of specific verses, often stressing the role of 'Ali ibn Abi Talib and the "People of the House," the blood relations of Muhammad.

Another sectarian deviation, in interpretation but not in text, is that of the Ahmadiyya, a nineteenth-century movement that began in the Indian province of the Punjab. The Ahmadis believe that their founder, Mirza Ghulam Ahmad (d. 1908), was a prophet, an assertion that runs directly counter to the mainstream Muslim belief that Muhammad is the final prophet. While they do not contest the textual integrity of the Qur'an, the Ahmadis propose divergent interpretation of certain verses. They reject, for example, the mainstream interpretation of Q 3:55 ("O Jesus! I am gathering you and causing you to ascend to Me"), which denies the death by crucifixion of Jesus but rather insist that Jesus died a natural death and will not return in a Second Coming.

Why do Muslims take a shower before touching the Qur'an?

Many religions require practices of ritual purification, and Islam is no exception. Q 56:77–79 declares: "That (this) is indeed a noble Qur'ān / In a book kept hidden / Which none touches except the purified." But who are "the purified"? A metaphorical interpretation of these verses might point to a believer's piety and spiritual preparedness. Read literally, however, they include the Qur'an within the scope of those objects and actions for which ablutions are required to render a person ritually clean and properly prepared for worship.

For a Muslim's prayer to be valid, the Qur'an mandates cleansing of specific body parts. Q 4:43 and Q 5:6 detail the requirements. There is some overlap between the two verses, but this is the most important passage: "O you who believe! When you rise up for prayer, wash your faces, and your hands up to the elbows, and lightly rub your heads and (wash) your feet up to the ankles. And if you are unclean, purify yourselves. And if you are sick or on a journey, or one of you comes from the toilet, or you have had contact with women, and you do not find water, then go to clean, high ground and rub your faces and your hands with some of it" (Q 5:6). The verse mentions some of the physical functions that render a person ritually impure, such as elimination and sexual intercourse. It also lists the body parts to be washed or wiped to restore purity.

Whether to wash or to wipe became, however, a ritual difference between Sunnis and Shi'is. Shi'is interpret the verse quoted in the previous paragraph (Q 5:6) to mandate the washing of faces and hands and the wiping of head and feet. Sunnis, however, understand it to require washing of faces, hands, and feet, while wiping suffices only for the head. This difference is not insignificant since improperly performed ablutions invalidate the prayer that follows them.

The books of Islamic law detail the technical terminology and precise requirements of ritual ablutions. These books characterize cleansing as either minor or major. Minor ablutions, the washings and wipings just described, must be done before praying or entering a mosque or picking up the Qur'an, if one has been asleep or has gone to the bathroom. Major ablutions that involve washing the entire body must be done after sexual intercourse, menstruation, and childbirth. Because non-Muslims do not perform these ritual cleansings, some stricter interpretations consider them to be in a permanent state of impurity and therefore unfit to enter a mosque or to touch an Arabic Qur'an.

The reverence with which Muslims treat the Qur'an has become a weapon in the hands of virulent Islamophobes. In the years immediately following September 11, 2001, accusations surfaced of Qur'an desecration being used in the interrogation of prisoners in Afghanistan and Iraq, as well as at Guantánamo Bay. The 2005 Newsweek report of one such incident at the Guantánamo detention camp provoked massive anti-US demonstrations in many parts of the Muslim world, some of which proved deadly. In 2011, a Florida pastor burned a Qur'an, sparking international outrage and condemnation by world leaders. Again, demonstrations and riots against this desecration resulted in dozens of deaths, both Muslim and non-Muslim.

PART II

MAJOR MESSAGES AND THEMES

Those who revere the Qur'an, those for whom it provides access to God's voice, find that it guides them in all aspects of their lives, not just the religious or spiritual parts. They learn about God and about how God wants humans to live, and they hear God directly in his own words. But they also come to understand the history of the cosmos, of the planet earth and its inhabitants, both humans and jinn, and of the natural environment. The Qur'an speaks about all of this and celebrates the created universe, from its largest sphere to its smallest speck, marking it as a manifold blessing for humans and as an inexhaustible set of signs that point them to their Creator.

Human social groupings, from the individual family unit to the entire Muslim community, form part of God's plan, and the Qur'an offers caution and encouragement to enhance harmonious relations at every level of social grouping. Since humans are sexual creatures, regulation of sexuality and of associations between those of different genders receive extensive treatment. Both as a community and as individuals, the Qur'an calls believers to a focus on the divine that expresses itself in periods of prayer, in prolonged fasting, in arduous pilgrimage, and in providing for the poor and bereft.

Prophets play a crucial role as transmitters of divine teachings who call their communities to accountability. The Qur'an acknowledges a long succession of prophets and messengers, culminating in God's final prophet, Muhammad. Earlier prophets, some known from the Bible and others from ancient Arabian lore, prefigure and pave the way for this "seal of the prophets." Their struggles and tribulations shape the qur'anic account of salvation history, manifesting God's work in the world with people of other times and places.

Recognizing the distinction between those who form part of the Muslim community and those who do not, the Qur'an addresses inter-religious contacts and connections, both positive and negative, as well as those that exist between Muslim and secular social units, whether tribes, nations, or the general category of unbelievers.

But, of course, the Qur'an is not a textbook on cosmology, or natural history, or sexuality and sociology, or government and international relations. While treating all of these subjects and many more, its aim is admonition, exhortation, and guidance. Put simply, through the words that he revealed to the Prophet Muhammad, God tells people, the humans whom he created, how to live. They are to recognize and worship him; they are charged, in the words of a well-known qur'anic phrase, with "commanding right and forbidding wrong," and if their good deeds outweigh their evil ones, they are promised an eternity of unimaginable delights.

4

GOD AND CREATION

What does the Qur'an say about God?

Some verses of the Qur'an are so important in Muslim thought and practice that they have been given names. One of these is Q 2:255, known as the "Throne Verse." It is worth repeating in full, for it captures essential elements of the qur'anic view of God's nature:

> God! There is no god except Him, the alive, the eternal. Neither slumber nor sleep overtakes Him. To Him belongs whatever is in the heavens and whatever is in the earth. Who is he that intercedes with Him except by His leave? He knows what is in front of them and what is behind them, while they encompass nothing of His knowledge except what He will. His throne includes the heavens and the earth, and He is never weary of preserving them. He is the sublime, the tremendous.

Above all, God is one. He is absolutely unique and nothing else shares in his singularity. The primary profession of faith in Islam begins "there is no god but God." From this perspective, Muslims find the Christian doctrine of the Trinity utterly indefensible. God cannot have a "son"; there cannot be "one God in three Persons." For Muslims such assertions are tantamount to blasphemy. God's glory is without limit and only God is worthy of worship. Consequently, giving to anything else the allegiance due only to God is the major sin.

Another important passage, Q 59:22–24, opens up aspects or attributes of the divine that are central to Muslim belief:

> He is God, than whom there is no other god, the knower of the invisible and the visible. He is the beneficent, the merciful.
>
> He is God, than whom there is no other god, the sovereign Lord, the holy one, peace, the keeper of faith, the guardian, the majestic, the compeller, the superb. Glorified be God from all that they ascribe as partner (to Him).
>
> He is God, the creator, the shaper out of nothing, the fashioner. His are the most beautiful names. All that is in the heavens and the earth glorifies Him, and He is the mighty, the wise.

If you look closely, you will find fifteen different descriptors for God in this passage. These, as well as many other characterizations that have been culled from the Qur'an, were compiled by Muslim theologians into lists of God's "most beautiful names," traditionally numbered as ninety-nine. Many Muslims use a circle of ninety-nine beads (or thirty-three counted thrice) to recite these names in prayer, a practice that has been called "the Islamic rosary."

God is creator of the heavens and the earth and human beings are the crown of his creation. Humans owe obedience and worship to God, and all of creation calls them to this through its beauties and wonders, both great and small. God guides his creation and, through the revelation of the Qur'an, clearly shows human beings how to live in accordance with his will. At the time of death, God judges each individual, weighing good deeds against evil and deciding whether eternity will be spent in Heaven or Hell.

While the qur'anic God is one of majesty and might, he is also a God of merciful intimacy. One of the best-loved verses speaks of this with a vivid, unforgettable image: "We created man and We know what his soul whispers to him, and We are nearer to him than his jugular vein" (Q 50:16).

Is the God of the Qur'an the same as the God of the Bible?

When an Arabic-speaking Christian opens her Bible, she will read: "In the beginning *Allah* created the heaven and the earth." *Allah* is the ordinary word for "God" in Arabic, and Middle Eastern Christians have been praying to Allah for centuries. Most linguists accept its etymology as a contraction of the definite article, *al*, and the word for divine being, *ilah*. They also note its relation to *El*, the Hebrew word for God, and *Elah*, the Aramaic version.

Yet many English-speaking Christians, particularly conservative Christians, resist and resent the idea of using the word "God" for the Muslim deity. They insist that Muslims and Christians are not praying to the same divine being. Conversely, an identical argument prompted a Malaysian court to rule in 2013 that it is illegal for non-Muslims to refer to God in the Malay language with the word "Allah." Behind such resistance lies a range of theological differences, all of which have been argued over for centuries in polemical debates between Christians and Muslims. Muslims accuse Christians of "tritheism"—believing in three gods (Father, Son, and Holy Spirit), thereby denying the utter divine uniqueness upon which Islamic monotheism insists. Despite continuous refutation by Christian theologians that "tritheism" is a caricature of the Christian doctrine of the Trinity, the accusation persists. Similarly, Christian assertions about Jesus as the Son of God and as fully human and fully divine make no sense to most Muslims. The Qur'an talks about Jesus and honors him as one of God's important prophets, but it resists deification of Jesus (or of Muhammad).

Some Christians, in turn, often depict the Muslim God as a God of law rather than a God of love. In reading the Qur'an, they find a God of anger and vengeance. All the common criticisms of Islam—the Prophet's polygamy and military aggression, the extreme corporal punishments, the poor treatment of women and religious minorities—are read as permitted or commanded by a deity quite other than the Christian God.

Particularly in recent decades, Muslims and Christians have grappled with these mutual misperceptions and have sought to find a common ground. While not denying differences between Islam and Christianity or between the biblical and qur'anic depictions of God, they search for the points of similarity, the places where bridges can be built between the two traditions. A major effort in this direction was the promulgation on October 18, 2007, of an open letter entitled "A Common Word between Us and You." The letter was addressed to Christian leaders around the world, such as the pope, the archbishop of Canterbury, the patriarch of Constantinople, and the general secretary of the World Council of Churches. It was signed by 138 Muslim scholars and religious leaders and has since been signed by hundreds more. Drawing its title from Q 3:64, "Say: O People of the Book! Come to a common word between us and you," this succinct document collects passages from the Bible and from the Qur'an that speak about love of God and love of neighbor. The point is to stress the similarities in Muslim and Christian understandings of God and to use those similarities as the basis for fruitful engagement between the two religions.

Does the Qur'an describe the creation of the world?

Throughout the Qur'an, God is invoked by such titles as the "Creator," the "One Who Originates," and the "Fashioner." All God need say is " 'Be' and it is" (Q 40:68, 2:117; 16:40, 36:82). The story of his initial creative act unfolds like the biblical narrative in Genesis 1. As in Genesis, the qur'anic account speaks of God creating heaven and earth in six days. Unlike the biblical story, however, God has no need of rest on the seventh day, nor does the Qur'an detail the specifics of each day's creative activity.

Humans stand as the first of all other creation, superior even to angels and jinn, because God breathed his own spirit into them (Q 38:73). As acknowledgment of this priority, the angels were commanded to prostrate themselves before Adam, and Adam is charged with stewardship of the earth. Humans also figure as central to the question of why God chose to create anything at all. The earth was designed to serve human needs, and its natural features and forces were shaped to that end. But God's creation is more than a human playground; it is also a testing field. As expressed in Q 18:7, "We have placed all that is in the earth as an ornament for it that we may try them: which of them is best in conduct."

While in multiple passages the Qur'an recounts the events through which the heavens and earth began, it also asserts God's ever-sustaining creative activity. As Q 2:255, the famous "Throne Verse" declares: "His throne includes the heavens and the earth, and He is never weary of preserving them." All creation, humankind included, depends on God for every instant of its existence. This continuous, life-sustaining generativity prompts some of the most beautiful passages in the Qur'an.

Many verses in the Qur'an urge humans to admire the natural world, to find in it "signs" of God's love and bounty, and to honor it as another form of his revelation. The Qur'an's use of the same word—*ayat* in Arabic—to signify these "signs" in nature and to denote its own individual verses creates a tight linguistic connection between these two forms of divine revelation, verbal and physical. The fiftieth sura of the Qur'an, known as the "Sura of Compassion," offers a lengthy recitation of God's creative blessings to humans. Deploying a frequent refrain ("Which is it, of the favors of your Lord, that you deny?") between the evocations of divine bounty, it has been likened to a qur'anic psalm.

The Qur'an makes clear that God has delegated responsibility for the earth to humans. That declaration, combined with this theology of the natural world as God's signs, provides a strong basis for Islamic environmental ethics. Humankind is charged with stewardship of the natural world, a world whose wonders and whose life-sustaining blessings are all signs that point to God the Creator.

How does the Qur'an talk about the natural world?

Hundreds of qur'anic verses celebrate the natural world as a sign of God's creative bounty. As just noted, creation happens because God says, "Be," and it is. In that primordial event, the sea and the dry land separated, mountains grounded and stabilized the earth, and rivers cut channels through it.

Above the earth, the sky or heavens arch over in seven successive layers (Q 2:29) and, at God's command, they serve humankind: "He makes the sun and the moon, constant in their courses, to be of service to you, and has made of service to you the night and the day" (Q 14:33). The sun and the moon, for example, provide a way to calculate the passage of days, months, and years. The stars guide the nighttime traveler on land or at sea. The all-encompassing value of the created world finds another confirmation in many formulaic oaths. Particularly in the earlier suras, the Qur'an testifies to the truth of its pronouncements with statements like "by the moon when she is at the full" (Q 84:18) or "by the star when it sets" (Q 53:1).

The twin themes of beauty and benefit also accrue to the qur'anic depiction of domesticated animals. God gave humans cattle not only for food and for warmth, but also for their loveliness: "in which is beauty for you, when you bring them home, and when you take them out to pasture" (Q 16:6). Q 16 goes on to speak of the burdens that such animals bear for their owners, adding horses, mules, and asses to the list.

Again, their beauty complements their benefit; they are both transportation and ornamentation (Q 16:8). This same sura, Q 16, takes its name from one of the tiniest creatures to which the Qur'an gives mention, the bee. Bees, too, serve humankind because "there comes forth from their bellies a drink diverse of hues, in which is healing for mankind" (Q 16:69).

The cycle of life and death functions as a frequent refrain in qur'anic statements about the natural world. Water is a source of life and regeneration. "And We send down from the sky blessed water whereby We give growth to gardens and the grain of crops / And lofty date-palms with ranged clusters" (Q 50:9–10). As new growth fades and dies in the sun's heat, rains return to revive the earth and repeat the cycle. Water in its multiple manifestations—seas, rivers, rainfall—figures in both earthly and heavenly blessings. The fountains and rivers of Paradise mirror and magnify all the benefits that water provides in the natural world.

From the earth's dirt itself, God forms the first humans, and to that dirt their bodies return at death. In all its descriptions of natural phenomena, the Qur'an underscores the invariable message of God's sublimity and sovereignty. All natural phenomena point to this, and gratitude must be the believer's response: "To Him belongs whoever is in the heavens and the earth. All are obedient to Him. / He it is who produces creation, then reproduces it, and it is easier for Him. His is the sublime similitude in the heavens and in the earth" (Q 30:26–27).

What is the relation of human beings to God and to nature?

Q 4:126 sets the fundamental principle of this relationship: "To God belongs whatever is in the heavens and whatever is in the earth. God ever surrounds all things." There is no separation between the created universe, the natural world, and God. God's oneness ensures the connectedness of creation. Humans are part of this unitary creation, but they are charged with a special responsibility for it. Humankind is called to be God's "caliph" on earth—a term that only later took on political connotations—and is charged with the oversight and care of all natural resources. Humans must act as God's trustees on earth. As already noted, the qur'anic and the biblical stories of creation overlap considerably. In both, God is the direct agent of creation. God fashions humans from the earth itself, from its dust or clay, forging an intimate relation between humans and the natural world.

The natural world nurtures and protects humans. Three verses in Q 14 beautifully express the concept of the natural environment as a divine gift:

> God is He Who created the heavens and the earth,
>   and causes water to descend from the sky, thereby
>   producing fruits as food for you, and makes the
>   ships to be of service to you, that they may run upon
>   the sea at His command, and has made the rivers of
>   service to you;
> And makes the sun and the moon, constant in their
>   courses, to be of service to you, and has made of
>   service to you the night and the day.
> And He gives you of all you ask of Him, and if you
>   would count the bounty of God you cannot reckon it.
>   (Q 14:32–34)

The final verse ends on a very different note—"Man is a wrong-doer, an ingrate"—a recognition that humans often refuse to recognize God's sovereignty over all his creation and try to make themselves like gods.

These verses, and many others like them, speak of how the natural world points humans to God. God makes his providence manifest through his acts in nature and in human beings. Such passages can be as simple as "And in the earth are portents for those whose faith is sure" (Q 51:20) or as lyrically constructed as:

And of His signs is this: He created for you spouses
   from yourselves that you might find rest in them,
   and He ordained between you love and mercy. In this
   indeed are signs for people who reflect.
And of His signs is the creation of the heavens and
   the earth, and the difference of your languages and
   colors. In this indeed are signs for men of knowledge.
And of His signs is your slumber by night and by day,
   and your seeking of His bounty. In this indeed are
   signs for people who heed.
And of His signs is this: He shows you the lightning for
   a fear and for a hope, and sends down water from the
   sky, and thereby quickens the earth after her death. In
   this indeed are signs for people who understand.
And of His signs is this: The heavens and the earth
   stand fast by His command, and afterward, when
   He calls you, from the earth you will emerge. (Q
   30:21–25)

Are there angels and devils in the Qur'an?

Q 35, entitled "The Angels," begins: "Praise be to God, the
creator of the heavens and the earth, who appoints the angels messengers having wings two, three and four." The
Qur'an frequently mentions angels, sometimes by names,
like Michael and Gabriel, which are familiar from the Bible.
Belief in angels is a core tenet of Muslim faith alongside belief in God, his books, his messengers, and his final judgment. Although angels preceded humans, the latter outrank
them, as conveyed in a compelling episode of the creation
narrative. In Q 2:30–34, angels question God's formation of
humans, fearing the negative consequences. Nevertheless,
God makes Adam and tells him, but not the angels, the
names of things. Later, when only Adam can provide these
names, God commands the angels to bow before him, and all
but one do so.

Angels carry messages from God to humans. Most importantly, Gabriel conveys the Qur'an to Muhammad: "Who is an enemy to Gabriel! For he it is who has revealed (this scripture) to your [Muhammad] heart by God's permission, confirming what was (revealed) before it, and a guidance and glad tidings to believers" (Q 2:97). Another passage speaks of Gabriel as Muhammad's protector and of the angels as his allies (Q 66:4).

In yet another set of messenger passages, the recipient is not Muhammad but Mary, the mother of Jesus. As with the Gospel narratives of the annunciation, Mary receives news of her pregnancy from angels when they give her "glad tidings of a word from Him, whose name is the Messiah, Jesus, son of Mary, illustrious in the world and the hereafter" (Q 3:42–48). A longer narrative of the annunciation and birth of Jesus found in the sura that bears Mary's name speaks of this angelic messenger as appearing in "the likeness of a perfect man" (Q 19:17).

Returning to the story of Adam's creation, recall the angel who refused to bow before him. God cursed this disobedient angel, identified as Iblis, with future punishment, but then delayed that sanction until Judgment Day. In the meantime, Iblis is allowed to roam the earth, leading the disbelievers astray. Some versions of the Adam story speak of the disobedient angel as Satan (*al-Shaytan* in Arabic), prompting commentators to suggest that Iblis was renamed after his insubordination. Q 18:51 inserts a further complication when it refers to Iblis not as a (fallen) angel but as "one of the jinn" who "rebelled against his Lord's command."

What are jinn?

In the Qur'an, jinn are an additional class of creatures alongside humans and angels. They are spirits created from fire. As Q 55:15 states: "And the jinn he created of smokeless fire." (In popular folktales and fairy stories, they are called genies.) While jinn can create mischief and lead people astray, they can guide people to do God's will and to follow the straight path. Q 72, entitled "The Jinn," begins with a story of jinn praising the Qur'an: "Say (O Muḥammad): 'It is revealed to me that a company of the jinn gave ear, and they said: 'We have heard a marvellous Qur'ān'" (Q 72:1).

5

REVELATION, PROPHECY, AND HISTORY

Why is Muhammad called both a prophet and a messenger?

The proper name "Muhammad" appears only four times in the Qur'an. Far more frequently, the Qur'an refers to Islam's founder as "prophet" or "messenger" or both. When combined, the term "messenger"—sometimes translated from the Arabic as "apostle"—comes first, a placement that may indicate a category of higher status. Classical Muslim interpreters of the Qur'an offer various explanations for the two designations. According to some, a messenger belongs to the subset of prophets who convey a revealed message or scripture to humans. Others characterize a messenger as one who brings a new religious law. Yet others define messengers as those who receive revelation from an angel. By contrast, they assert that revelation comes to prophets only in dreams. The categories sometimes overlap, as in the case of Muhammad, as well as that of Moses.

But not every messenger is a prophet, nor is every messenger a human being. For example, Q 35 begins, "Praise be to God, the creator of the heavens and the earth, who appoints the angels messengers having wings two, three and four." An angel informed Abraham that he would have a son. Q 6:61 refers to the angels who safeguard humans and receive their souls when they die.

Prophets and messengers are among God's blessing to their respective peoples, and they serve an essential function for human life on earth. When God expelled Adam and his wife from the Garden of Eden, he promised that they would be instructed about how to live as God wills. Q 2:38 proclaims this promise: "We said: 'Go down, all of you, from here; but there comes to you from Me a guidance; and whoever follows My guidance, no fear shall come upon them neither shall they grieve.'"

The major prophets who fall into the category of those who received divine revelation and who brought a religious law are Adam, Noah, Abraham, Moses, Jesus, and Muhammad. According to Muslim tradition, many more prophets—the number is sometimes given as 124,000—do not bring a revelation and law but convey God's will to their peoples in their own languages. The notion of a lineage or legacy of prophetic revelation is expressed in verses like Q 3:3: "He has revealed to you (Muhammad) the scripture with truth, confirming what was (revealed) before it, even as He revealed the Torah and the Gospel."

What other prophets appear in the Qur'an?

Names like Abraham, Noah, Moses, and Jesus appear frequently in the Qur'an. Their stories, and those of other biblical prophets, weave narrative threads throughout the text and provide an important argument for the legitimacy of Mohammad's prophethood. In the qur'anic telling, Muhammad is but the latest in a long line of divinely directed prophets and messengers. His status, therefore, is neither unprecedented nor unique, as Q 46:9 states, "Say: 'I am no new thing among the messengers (of God) . . .'" and Q 3:144 affirms, "Muhammad is but a messenger, messengers (the like of whom) have passed away before him." This assertion of Muhammad's prophetic lineage and spiritual linkage to earlier prophets connects the Qur'an to previously revealed scriptures. All scriptures in this successive chain of revelations are equal and compel the believers' assent: "Say (O Muslims): 'We believe in God and what is revealed to us and what was revealed to Abraham, and Ishmael, and Isaac, and Jacob, and the tribes, and what Moses and Jesus received, and what the prophets received from their Lord. We make no distinction among any of them, and to Him we have surrendered.'"

Q 42:13 further underscores the unity of prophets and their messages: "He has ordained for you that religion which He commended to Noah, and what We inspire in you (Muhammad), and what We commended to Abraham and Moses and Jesus. . . ." All prophets call their people to the observance of God's unitary guidance. God's religion, Islam, is singular, and the prophets have proclaimed this religion in their preaching and in their persistent refutation of polytheism and idolatry. In Q 41:5 (and, similarly, in Q 18:110): "Say (to them, O Muhammad): 'I am only a mortal like you. It is inspired in me that your god is one God, therefore take the straight path to Him and seek forgiveness of Him. And woe to the idolaters.'"

But such prophetic exhortations were rarely well received. Rather than obediently acknowledging the rightness of these revealed messages, people repeatedly rebuked and disdained their prophets. They ridiculed them, called them liars, and dismissed them as ordinary folk with outrageous ideas. So persistent was this pattern that an entire group of qur'anic narratives can claim the category of "punishment stories." An interesting parallel to this pattern appears in the biblical book known as 2 Chronicles: "The Lord, the God of their fathers, sent persistently to them by his messengers, because he had compassion on his people and on his dwelling place / but they kept mocking the messengers of God, despising his words, and scoffing at his prophets, till the wrath of the Lord rose against his people, till there was no remedy" (2 Chronicles 36:15–16).

The stories replicate a simple threefold structure: a prophet or messenger preaches God's will and guidance to his people;

the people rebuke and reject him; God punishes the unrepentant people with destruction. Although biblical prophets feature prominently in these stories, nonbiblical prophets do as well. These latter are figures like Hud, Salih, and Shu'ayb, whom the Qur'an presents as drawn from ancient Arabian lore. While the punishment stories function primarily as a divine warning of the chastisement that will afflict those who reject God's guidance, they also serve as a form of encouragement for the Prophet Muhammad (and his followers), summoning him to perseverance in the face of adversity. By repeatedly reminding Muhammad of the rejection suffered by previous prophets and messengers, the divine voice in the Qur'an promises his final vindication and the triumph of his community. According to Q 11:120, "And all that We relate to you of the story of the messengers is in order that by it We may make firm your heart."

Does the Qur'an mention historical events?

Although most contemporary non-Muslim historians contest the claim, the Qur'an presents itself as conveying actual historical events and well-established facts. As with other religious scriptures such as the Bible, God is invoked as the ultimate validator of these claims. But also as with the Bible, that does not satisfy the secular scholar who wants to find the antecedents. Much current work on the Qur'an seeks to uncover its possible connections with earlier literatures of the Middle East, such as biblical narratives themselves and Syriac liturgical texts. While specific linkages remain elusive, clearly the Qur'an reflects an integration or awareness of such material. Additional narrative streams derive from ancient Arabian sources—lengthy genealogies and accounts of fabled battles—as well as south Arabian chronicles of past events.

The qur'anic sense of chronology, like the biblical, looks back to the inaugural events of creation. The six days of the world's creation (Q 11:7; 57:4) usher in the era of human history and of the human-divine relationship. This foundational story departs from the biblical version in several respects. While there are no details about Eve's creation or the issuance of a post-Paradise curse, there is a divine command that the angels prostrate themselves before Adam, a command that Satan refused. The truth of these events, and of many others familiar from the biblical sources, is repeatedly proclaimed. As human history begins to unfold in the stories about Noah, Abraham, Moses, and other prophets, the moral lessons to be drawn are always foregrounded. Joseph and his brothers, the exile to Egypt, the plagues and punishments visited upon the Egyptians—all of these are presented as both historical reality and as God's direct action in history. Reflection upon them should guide the believers in their behavior to God and each other.

References to these events can be found throughout the text, but rarely in the form of a sustained, developed narrative. The exceptions are the story of Joseph, to which the entire twelfth sura is devoted, and a shorter narrative not found in the Bible but popular in Christian circles, that of the Seven Sleepers. That the prophets mentioned in the Qur'an, continuing with figures like Solomon, David, and, finally, Jesus, were real historical figures is never questioned in the qur'anic text. They constitute a chain of divine messengers sent to straighten the course of history with their unified message about the one God and his guidance and goodwill for humankind.

Hints of historical personages operating far from more local contexts appear, for example, in the story of Moses and a mysterious "two-horned" figure whom commentators have regularly identified as Alexander the Great. For events just before or contemporary with Muhammad's lifetime, Q 30 provides a prime example with its reference to the Byzantines (al-Rum in Arabic) for whom the sura is named. Within the Arabian Peninsula itself, allusions to ancient Arabian peoples of the northern regions, such as Thamud and the peoples to whom the prophets Hud and Salih were sent, are complemented by those that touch south Arabia and neighboring Abyssinia (Ethiopia). Notable in this category is the detailed account of the Queen of Sheba and her relations with King Solomon.

Post-qur'anic commentary considerably expands the connections that Islamic scholarship has drawn between qur'anic allusions and historical events in the past, in the future, and in the lifetime of the Prophet. As biographies of Muhammad emerged in the centuries after his death, these connections became enshrined in the expanded historical memory of the Muslim world.

6

BEHAVIOR AND JUDGMENT

*What does the Qur'an say about death and life
after death?*

For pre-Islamic Arabs, fate was the agent of death, and the
only immortality lay in the memories of one's tribal kin.
Muhammad, however, preached a very different view of death
and its aftermath. Suddenly his listeners were presented with
images of a new life beyond the grave, a life vastly more en-
joyable than that of this earthly realm. This concept of a life
after death shaped every aspect of life on earth. Both life and
death are divine gifts, wholly under the determination of God.
God gives life by breathing his spirit into the human form and
withdraws this spirit at the moment of death. It is precisely
God's power over death that is the most compelling qur'anic
argument for his existence. Muhammad promises that resurrection and life after death should nullify the fear of death, but
only for those whose lives can successfully pass the final divine judgment.

With the promise of Paradise (or Hell), life becomes a testing
ground, a period in which belief in God can be demonstrated
through righteous and pious acts. God's power over death, in
Islam as well as in other prophetic religions, is understood as
a liberating force, freeing humans from the grip of fate and
producing a new creation. Humans who live in submission
and service to their Creator can anticipate an eternal life with

God. When Muslims first hear about a death, they often respond with "to God we belong and to him is our return," a phrase from Q 2:156. When the family realizes that death is approaching, they will often whisper the confession of faith (*shahada* in Arabic) in the dying person's ear and recite verses of the Qur'an, such as those from Q 36, that speak about the final resurrection.

While the Qur'an says little about the moment of death itself, the books of hadith provide ample elaboration. For example, they talk about the angel, 'Azra'il, who takes souls at the moment of death, and the two other angels, Munkar and Nakir, who question the deceased in the grave to confirm her unwavering belief in God, Muhammad, and Islam.

Islamic law and practice prescribe burial for the body of the deceased. This should be done promptly, but not before the corpse has been carefully washed and wrapped in a shroud. Certain funeral prayers accompany the burial, and the body must be interred facing the direction of the Meccan Ka'ba. The Qur'an presents internment as a prelude to the resurrection: "Then causes him to die, and buries him; then, when He will, He brings him again to life" (Q 80:21–22). Special blessings accrue to the deceased with the recitation of particular qur'anic verses and, in many Muslim cultures, the family invites friends and relatives to memorial events in the home, mosque, or assembly hall that feature trained Qur'an reciters.

Many Muslims believe that after death the soul enters *barzakh*, an Arabic term that can be translated as "barrier"— Q 23:100 speaks of "a barrier until the day when they are raised"—and which is often understood as obstructing any contact between the dead and the living. While the living can pray for the dead, the dead can make no response and must abide in their graves until the final resurrection.

The Qur'an has much to say about the Day of Judgment, the final resurrection, and one's ultimate destination in Heaven or Hell. The inevitaly of a final reckoning for all one's earthly actions stands as a key feature of Muhammad's preaching.

Whether it is called "the last day," "the hour," or "the day of decision," descriptions of this ultimate point in human history abound. A traditional list of twelve signs, drawn from the Qur'an and the hadith, presage the end times, the precise moment of which God alone knows. Q 39:68 signals a dramatic start: "And the trumpet is blown. . . . Then it is blown a second time, and behold them standing waiting!" What the resurrected await is judgment. Each will be given a book with all of life's actions recorded. Those whose books are placed in their right hand will go to Heaven; those who receive their books in the left hand are bound for Hell.

Are there descriptions of Heaven and Hell?

Few aspects of Muslim belief have captured popular consciousness like the depictions of Heaven and of the rewards that Heaven will offer. While these portrayals find further elaboration in post-qur'anic literature, the Qur'an itself has much to say on the subject. As with the biblical Genesis, life's final abode is presented as a garden, a reference to be found well over a hundred times in the Qur'an. Other names are given, such as Paradise or Eden or the Hereafter, and Q 55:46 even refers to two gardens. Subsequent commentaries detail the size, shape, and ranking of all these references.

But who dwells in these gardens? Who enjoys the everlasting delights that abound there? The primary and primordial inhabitant is, of course, God. With him dwell his angels, and Q 13:23 describes how they will welcome the righteous, those who have earned this eternal reward by living their lives according to God's will.

Q 56, "The Event," speaks extensively about the Last Day, Heaven, and Hell and details the delights promised to "those of the right hand," that is, those who received the record of their earthly deeds in their right hands because their good deeds outweighed their wrongdoings. They will recline on luxurious couches and be served drink from a pure spring "from which they get no aching of the head nor any madness" (Q 56:19). They will be fed with the finest fruits and the "flesh of fowls that they desire" (Q 56:21). Their companions will be "fair ones with wide, lovely eyes" (Q 56:22).

The site of such pleasures is a glorious garden through which four rivers flow, rivers of water, of milk, of honey, and of wine that does not intoxicate. A plenitude of shaded bowers, a bounty of food and drink served on exquisite tableware, and an endless supply of beautiful, virtuous women justify the qur'anic description of Paradise as "all that souls desire and eyes find sweet" (Q 43:71).

Beyond the bodily pleasures of Paradise lie the much more enthralling joys of the spirit. In never-ending bliss, the believer basks in the presence of God, praising him without end and gazing upon his glorious countenance. As Q 75:22–23 assures the faithful, "That day will faces be resplendent, looking toward their Lord." The belief that in Heaven one would gaze on God was not, however, without controversy. Some theologians argued against the obvious anthropomorphism of this assertion, insisting that the divine presence, invisible but spiritually perceived, would be the overwhelming rapture of Paradise.

Special account is taken of those who die as martyrs. Many interpret Q 47:4–6 as a guarantee that martyrs are ushered immediately into God's presence: "And those who are slain in the way of God, He does not render their actions vain. / He will guide them and improve their state, / And bring them in to the Garden which He has made known to them."

Graphic depictions of heavenly gratifications are matched by equally vivid renderings of Hell's horrors. Those whose evil deeds in this life outweigh their good are flung into an endless fire. This includes disbelievers, apostates, and idolaters. As a mirroring counterpart to heavenly joys, Hell torments the damned with food and drink that disgusts and sickens, and with companions of equal depravity. And their torments will never end: "Whoever comes guilty to his Lord, for him is hell. There he will neither die nor live" (Q 20: 74). Some theologians, however, questioned whether Hell is indeed eternal. They argued that nothing other than God can be eternal, or that God's justice requires that he could assign a period of punishment commensurate with human offenses but would then offer a final release.

Is it true that the Qur'an promises a Paradise of virgins?

Depictions of Paradise in the Qur'an often surprise people with their vivid sensuality. And, yes, there are virgins to welcome the (male) believers in Paradise. But let's back up a bit and sketch the larger context. As just noted, Heaven—or Paradise, or the Garden(s), or Eden, or the Abode of Peace—is a real, physical place where living human beings enjoy a bounty of pleasures unmatched by anything on earth. The people welcomed to this celestial abode have earned their entry. They lived virtuous lives marked by good deeds, fear of God and his judgment, prayer and worship, and care and support for the poor and needy. Q 4:122–124 sums this up: "But as for those who believe and do good works We shall bring them into gardens underneath which rivers flow, in which they will abide forever."

This mention of rivers can open the discussion of the pleasure and delights of Paradise. The phrase "rivers of Paradise" occurs almost fifty times in the Qur'an. It conjures up a lush, verdant environment, an endless oasis of bountiful vegetation—trees to offer cooling cover, flowering plants of beautiful hues, and luscious fruits of every variety. The rivers offer pure refreshing water but also other libations: "rivers of unpolluted water, and rivers of milk of which the flavor does not change, and rivers of wine delicious to the drinkers, and rivers of clear-run honey" (Q 47:15).

Within this tranquil setting, the blessed recline on soft couches, clothed in silk garments, eating fruits from golden trays and drinking wine from crystal goblets, all offered by servants passing among them. For male believers, that phrase includes "wide-eyed maidens" (*houris*) "of modest gaze, whom neither man nor jinn will have touched" (Q 55:56). The houris are compared to hidden pearls (Q 56:23) who bring unceasing delight. While the qur'anic mentions of this promised pleasure are somewhat restrained, the hadith expand and elaborate upon the Qur'an's spare comments. It is from the hadith that popular lore about the houris has built images, for example, of martyrs wed to seventy-two—or five hundred or a thousand— virgins, each of whom never ages and never loses her virginity. According to some scholars, the promise of the Paradise virgins as a motivation for holy war (jihad) can be found as early as the eighth century and continues through the medieval and into the modern periods of Islamic history.

The emphasis on physical, sensual pleasures that has long been associated with the Muslim Paradise often overshadows, in the popular imagination, the profound spiritual pleasures. Foremost among these are the joys of the divine presence and the everlasting, all-pervading peace. Both in the early and in the contemporary periods of Islam, excessive emphasis on the sensual pleasures of Paradise—an emphasis that has often found its way into anti-Islamic polemical literature—has troubled many Muslims. Some prefer to interpret the physical manifestations as metaphors for the unbounded generosity that God will offer his faithful for all eternity. Others, while not denying the reality of Heaven's physical delights, prefer to focus on the overriding glory of the divine presence.

Does the Qur'an contain commandments? Is it a law book?

Few elements of the Judeo-Christian tradition are more well-known than the Ten Commandments. An image of Moses holding the tablets of the Ten Commandments can be found on the eastern pediment of the US Supreme Court.

Looking for a qur'anic equivalent, some commentators start with Q 7:145 and its reference to God's writing for Moses "upon the tablets, the lesson to be drawn from all things and the explanation of all things." The eighteen verses of Q 17:22–39 offer similar injunctions to those found in the Ten Commandments, although most scholars see such a list as representing a common store of ethical wisdom, rather than a direct borrowing from the Bible. Here are some excerpts from that long passage:

> Your Lord has decreed, that you worship none save
>   Him, and (that you show) kindness to parents. (23)
> Give the kinsman his due, and the needy, and the
>   wayfarer, and do not squander (your wealth) in
>   wantonness. (26)
> And do not come near to adultery. It is an abomination
>   and an evil way. (32)
> Fill the measure when you measure, and weigh with a
>   right balance; that is fitting, and better in the end. (35)
> (O man), do not follow that of which you have no
>   knowledge. The hearing and the sight and the
>   heart—of each of these it will be asked. (36)
> And do not walk in the earth exultant. You cannot rend
>   the earth, nor can you stretch to the height of the
>   hills. (37)
> And do not set up with God any other god, for fear that
>   you be cast into hell, reproved, abandoned. (39)

A summary of this list in Q 6:152–154 concludes with the admonition, "and (He commands you, saying): This is My straight path, so follow it."

People often think of the Qur'an as the Muslim law code. Just as a frieze in the Supreme Court enshrines Moses displaying the Ten Commandments, it depicts Muhammad holding the Qur'an. Like the Hebrew Bible, the Qur'an does contain legal prescriptions, but cumulatively they represent a small portion of the text. Nevertheless, the Qur'an stands as a primary source of Islamic law, and the interpretation of its prescriptive and proscriptive verses constitutes a special genre of qur'anic commentaries. The specificity of certain verses creates a challenge to contemporary considerations of human rights. For example, a literal reading of passages that decree flogging for fornication or amputation for thievery has shaped the penal codes of some Muslim countries, while many others follow less restrictive interpretations or have adopted civil and criminal codes drawn from European legal systems.

Do people determine their behavior or does God?

The belief that all events are predetermined and that human life is controlled by fate has very ancient roots. When translated into a theological context, this belief raises the question of how to balance the acknowledgment of divine omnipotence with the possibility of human free will. Those Arabs who were the first recipients of Muhammad's preaching lived and died under the sway of an impersonal fate or destiny. All the events of one's lifetime, the moments of birth and death, as well as every individual action and its consequences, were predetermined. There was no escape from what an irresistible destiny had foreordained.

Exposure to the Prophet's preaching of the qur'anic revelation altered this belief for the nascent Muslim community. An omnipotent divine being, the creator and lord of all, replaced fate as the decisive force in human existence. Passages in the Qur'an directly refute the pre-Islamic notion of an impersonal destiny. Instead of fate (identified as time), it is God who "gives life to you, then causes you to die, then gathers you to the day of resurrection" (Q 45:26). This God knows everything. His omniscience is all-encompassing, subsuming all aspects of created reality: "And He knows what is in the land and the sea. Not a leaf falls but He knows it, not a grain amid the darkness of the earth, nothing of wet or dry but (it is noted) in a clear record" (Q 6:59). The next verse speaks of "the term appointed to you," echoing the ancient belief that even the time of one's death is preordained.

A number of verses reinforce this concept of predestination with statements like "God sends whom He will astray, and guides whom He will" (Q 14:4; 13:27; 74:31). One repetition of this even connects God's complete control to the diversity of human society: "Had God willed He could have made you (all) one nation, but He sends whom He will astray and guides whom He will" (Q 16:93).

Yet, in Q 9:51, Muhammad is urged to say to believers that "[n]othing befalls us except what God has decreed for us. He is our protecting friend. In God let believers put their trust!" So benevolence must be added to the attributes of God. But doesn't that complicate the question of predestination? Many theologians of the eighth and ninth centuries certainly thought so. They posed the question in terms of the last judgment. If human beings will be judged for their earthly actions, with Heaven and Hell as the consequences of this judgment, don't people have to be responsible for what they do (or fail to do)? One group of Muslim thinkers who became prominent in Shi'i thought insisted that a just God could not condemn people unless they could control their deeds. They point to passages like Q 18:29–32 that promise Paradise to those who "believe and do good works" and Hell to those who willfully disbelieve.

No decisive or unequivocal answer can be drawn from the Qur'an alone. It remains a theological conundrum, with most of the Muslim tradition leaning toward predestination but with significant voices raised in every century to support the position of human freedom and responsibility.

If people sin, can they repent and be forgiven?

The ninth sura of the Qur'an carries the title "Repentance" and the many verses in the Qur'an that treat this topic convey notions of reciprocity. The sinner returns to God and God then turns toward the penitent: "But whoever repents after his wrongdoing and amends, God will relent toward him. God is forgiving, merciful" (Q 5:39). Numerous examples repeat this pattern of mutual dependence between repentance and God's merciful forgiveness. The human returns to God from sin, and God turns back to the penitent with forgiveness.

Don't wait too long, however, the Qur'an cautions. Some chilling verses depict the fate of those who postpone their repentance until it is too late. Finding themselves among the dammed, they cry out: "Our Lord! We have now seen and heard, so send us back; we will do right, now we are sure" (Q 32:12). But there is no going back and, as Q 35:37 forebodingly proclaims, "evil-doers have no helper."

Precedents from the past underscore the qur'anic message about seeking God's pardon. The Qur'an puts many stories of repentance before the believers. Some involve ancient peoples, while others feature their prophets. In examples that will be familiar from the Hebrew Bible, the Israelites beg for forgiveness after creating the golden calf (Q 7:148–149) and the people of Jonah return to God after their sin (Q 10:99). Pre-Islamic prophets like Moses, David, and Solomon are lauded for seeking God's forgiveness for even minor indiscretions, as when Moses repents his request to see the face of God (Q 7:143). The first qur'anic prophet, Adam, stands as a prototype of repentance and forgiveness. When Adam and Eve eat the fruit of the forbidden tree, they plead: "Our Lord! We have wronged ourselves. If You do not forgive us and do not have mercy on us, surely we are of the lost!" (Q 7:23). Muslim theologians square this narrative with the theological conviction that prophets are sinless by asserting that Adam's vocation as a prophet begins only with his expulsion from Paradise.

Just as God forgives those who express sincere repentance, believers are to forgive each other: "Let them forgive and show indulgence. Do you not yearn that God may forgive you?" (Q 24:22). Aligned with forgiveness, in certain situations, are acts of atonement, efforts to make amends for offense or injury. An instance that can invoke atonement would be failing to fast during the month of Ramadan or breaking that fast for a period of time. Q 2:184 allows makeup days for those who do not observe Ramadan because of illness or travel. Alternatively, one can feed a poor person to atone for not fasting because circumstances prevent it. In Q 2:196, similar forms of compensation are required of those who cannot make the pilgrimage to Mecca (*hajj* in Arabic) or who must interrupt their hajj.

Does the Qur'an predict the end of the world? Who is the Antichrist?

The Qur'an says a lot about what will happen when the world ends and offers vivid and terrifying descriptions of the cataclysmic events that will signal that end. Muhammad's early preaching presented an urgent call to personal and social reform because God would hold us to a final accounting with eternal reward or punishment as the consequence. For Muhammad's first listeners, the concepts of bodily resurrection, life after death, and a decisive judgment on one's earthly deeds were alien and unwelcome. Many laughed at these ideas, muttering derisively, "When we are bones and fragments shall we be raised up as a new creation?" (Q 17:98).

A mighty trumpet blast will announce the end: "And the trumpet is blown, and all who are in the heavens and the earth swoon away, save him whom God wills. Then it is blown a second time, and behold them standing waiting!" (Q 39:69). When this happens, "the earth with the mountains shall be lifted up and crushed with one crash," "the heaven will split asunder" and eight angels will hold the throne of God aloft (Q 69:14–17). Only God knows when this will happen. It will come suddenly and take people by surprise.

Bodies will rise from the graves and rejoin their spirits. All creatures will gather and stand together awaiting individual judgment. Many names are given to this event: the day of resurrection, the last day, the day of decision, the day of reckoning. No one escapes this final accounting; every single individual will be judged. A person's "book of deeds" plays a critical role. This book registers every human action or thought, whether good or bad. If the book is placed in the right hand of the resurrected person, Heaven awaits. If placed in the left hand, he is bound for Hell. Another image and instrument is the "balance," with evil deeds piled on one side of the scale and good on the other: "Then, as for him whose scales are heavy (with good works) / He will live a pleasant life. / But as for him whose scales are light, [the destiny is] / Raging fire" (Q 101:6–11).

As with so many other matters, the Prophet's hadith and the commentaries of classical Muslim scholars elaborate and enlarge all of these apocalyptic events. In particular, Sunni literature about the end times defines a place for Jesus as the one who will defeat the Antichrist, known as *Dajjal* in Arabic, and inaugurate a reign of peace before the world ends.

In Shi'i Islam this role is played by the Mahdi, a messianic figure who vanished in 874 CE but remains hidden in the world. His return will restore justice to the earth, a concept that has played an important role in various reformist efforts, especially in the nineteenth and twentieth centuries.

7

RELIGIOUS REQUIREMENTS

Why do Muslims pray five times a day?

Many visitors to Muslim countries retain the memory of witnessing large crowds of people praying in public spaces or in the streets around overflowing mosques. They will have seen the physical postures of ritual prayer as men stand together in neat rows and then bow and prostrate themselves in unison. Five times a day, this scene is repeated as Muslims perform the ritual prayer known as *salat* in Arabic.

Prostration in prayer powerfully demonstrates human adoration of the divine. "O you who believe! Bow down and prostrate yourselves, and worship your Lord" (Q 22:77). Each of the daily prayer periods, whose precise performance varies somewhat, includes this act of dropping to the knees and leaning forward to place one's forehead on the ground. It symbolizes the self-abnegation of the creature before the Creator.

Muslims pray because the Qur'an commands it: "There is no god but Me. So serve Me and establish worship for My remembrance" (Q 20:14). According to Q 51:56, God built this desire to worship him into the very nature of his creation.

Whether done at home or in a communal space, there are specific times mandated for the daily ritual prayer: at daybreak (*fajr*), the noon hour (*dhuhr*), middle of the afternoon ('*asr*), just after sunset (*maghrib*), and at nightfall ('*isha*). While

Sunni Muslims observe *salat* as five different prayer periods, Shi'i Muslims combine the noon and the afternoon prayers and the sunset and nightfall prayers.

In Muslim countries, the day's rhythms are marked by the public call to prayer, as the familiar (usually recorded) voice of the muezzin broadcasts from the towers (minarets) of neighborhood mosques. The slightly different timing of these broadcasts can create a cascading cacophony of sound that echoes through towns and villages. In non-Islamic countries, Muslims must rely on their watches or, increasingly, on smartphone apps to keep track of prayer times and to indicate the precise orientation to Mecca.

Establishing that direction is one of the preparatory practices for prayer. Another is washing or wiping particular parts of the body, such as the hands, feet, and head, or even taking a bath or shower. For prayer to be valid, the devotee must be in a state of ritual purity.

As one might imagine, trying to observe these ritual requirements in a non-Muslim country can be challenging. For the most part, American workplaces and work schedules are not designed to accommodate religious observances. Even more problematic is the negative perception in this country of public prayer as a sign of terrorist intent. Muslims have been penalized and even arrested for such behavior.

Friday, rather than Saturday (Judaism) or Sunday (Christianity), is the day of communal prayer gathering in Islam. The weekly congregational prayer at the local mosque includes a sermon that often draws upon qur'anic passages to emphasize moral and ethical issues. In most American mosques, like those in the Muslim world, men and women pray in separate sections. Either women stand in rows behind the men, or they are relegated to a separate room. Women in the United States, and elsewhere, have begun to agitate against this gender segregation, particularly when the separate room is a decidedly substandard space. Many younger, American-educated Muslims avoid mosque participation as a form of resistance to gender inequity, preferring to pray at home or in more equitable communal spaces. A few years ago, a women-only mosque community was launched in Los Angeles. The Women's Mosque of America maintains an active website (https://womensmosque.com/) and sponsors monthly congregational prayer services.

Does the Qur'an say that Muslims must fast for an entire month?

Once a year, Muslims fast for a full month. The rules for the proper observance are quite specific. During the daylight hours, adults must abstain from eating any food, from having anything to drink (even water), and from engaging in sexual relations. The month designated for the observance is Ramadan, the ninth month of the Islamic calendar.

Why was that particular month chosen? Q 2:183 makes the link: "The month of Ramaḍan in which was revealed the Qur'ān, a guidance for mankind, and clear proofs of the guidance, and the criterion (of right and wrong). And whoever of you is present, let him fast the month." The connection between Ramadan and the Qur'an's revelation sanctifies this month. In this passage, reference is being made not to the years-long sequential disclosure of the Qur'an, but to its "descent" from the lowest heaven on the Night of Power, an event commemorated during the final days of Ramadan. The last ten days of the month have particular importance because they memorialize this divine gift of the Qur'an's revelation. A special day, the "Night of Power" is usually celebrated on the 27th by Sunnis and the 23rd by Shi'is. It commemorates the Qur'an's full "descent" and the revelation of the Qur'an's first verses. On those dates, some Muslims keep a night-long prayer vigil at the mosque or at home. On other dates during Ramadan, Shi'is honor the birth or death dates of their first two imams, 'Ali ibn Abi Talib, Muhammad's cousin and son-in-law, and Hasan ibn 'Ali, the son of 'Ali and of Muhammad's daughter, Fatima.

The month of Ramadan begins with the sighting of the new moon, but Muslim groups differ on whether this must be a visual sighting or whether astronomical calculations will suffice. Individuals ordinarily follow the guidance of the local mosque, although some may choose to align their practice with other organizations or groups.

Paradoxically, the month of fasting is also a month of feasting, often communal feasting. The rigors of the fast strengthen the spiritual lives of believers, and the evening meals that break the day's fast, whether at the local mosque or at the homes of friends and relatives, cement the ties of care and friendship within the Muslim community. To prepare their homes for the family and guests that they will welcome during Ramadan, many people decorate in ways similar to what Christians do for Christmas and Jews do for Hanukkah.

Mosques feature special programs during the month, including extra prayers after the regular night prayer, Qur'an recitation sessions, community dinners, and religious lectures. In addition to being apportioned into chapters (suras) and verses, the Qur'an is divided into thirty equal parts to facilitate its full recitation during the month of Ramadan. Most copies of the Arabic Qur'an carry notations in the margins to mark these divisions.

Ramadan fasting concludes with a major festival of the Islamic religious calendar, 'Id al-Fitr. Like the festival days of many other religious traditions, 'Id al-Fitr entails special decorations for the house, the purchase of new clothes, the preparation of lavish meals, and the exchange of greetings ("have a blessed festival" or 'Id Mubarak in Arabic) and visits.

The example of a prolonged fast followed by a communal festival can also be found in the Christian practice of the forty-day Lenten fast that culminates in the celebration of Jesus's resurrection on Easter. In its contemporary observance, however, the Lenten fast does not approach the rigor of Ramadan. Remember, because the months of the Islamic calendar rotate around the Western Gregorian calendar, Ramadan will occur in all four seasons during the lifetime of an individual. Imagine observing the fast during the hot summer in Saudi Arabia or Sudan, going without anything to drink or eat from sunrise to sunset.

Is pilgrimage to Mecca mentioned in the Qur'an?

Every year about two million Muslims converge on a single spot in western Saudi Arabia. They come from all over the world, undertaking an often arduous journey. This spot is Mecca, the most sacred site in Islam. Making a pilgrimage to Mecca—*hajj* in Arabic—at least once in a lifetime represents one of the essential religious duties for all Muslims. Q 3:97 provides the key passage: "And pilgrimage to the House is a duty to God for mankind, for he who can find a way there." "House" is understood as the sanctuary of Mecca and the phrase "who can find a way there" qualifies the requirement. It means that a pilgrimage to Mecca must be completed only by those who have the physical stamina and the financial resources to do so.

The pilgrimage comprises a series of ritual activities that can only be validly performed during a five-day period in the twelfth and final month of the Islamic year. The Islamic calendar is lunar, with twelve months of between twenty-nine and thirty days each, totaling about eleven days less than the Western solar calendar of 365 days. Consequently, the months of the Islamic calendar shift through all of the seasons in a cycle of just over thirty-two years. Given this variability, sometimes the pilgrimage month falls during the winter and sometimes it occurs in full summer, making the experience much more difficult.

Most pilgrims arrive by air, and the Saudi government has built a special terminal for them at the airport in Jeddah. Because many more Muslims wish to make the pilgrimage each year than can be accommodated in Mecca and its surrounding sites, the Saudi government puts a cap on the number of visas given to residents of a given country, with the number of visas proportional to the percentage of the world's Muslim population the particular country contains. Understandably, the most populous Muslim countries (e.g., Indonesia, India, Pakistan, and Bangladesh) receive the most visas, and each country has a system of internal distribution.

Having arrived in Jeddah to begin the hajj, pilgrims perform special ablutions to enter a state of ritual purity, and men wrap themselves in two lengths of white cloth as a sign of this sanctification. (Many will save these clothes for their burial.) While women do not have a prescribed form of dress, they wear modest clothing, leaving their hands and face uncovered.

Proceeding into the sacred precincts, pilgrims chant over and over, "Here I am, Lord! Here I am!" as they approach Mecca and the Ka'ba. Then they journey to Mina, a site about five miles from Mecca, where they will sleep in tents (from basic to luxurious). From there, the next stop is the Plain of Arafat for a day-long period of prayer and reflection. A further stop at Muzdalifa precedes the return to Mina for the casting of stones and the sacrificial feast day of 'Id al-Adha. Upon return to Mecca, pilgrims walk seven times around the Ka'ba, starting at the corner that holds the Black Stone. Finally, they run, also seven times, between the two small hills of Safa and Marwa.

While not many verses in the Qur'an deal with the pilgrimage, certain passages have become associated with elements of the full pilgrimage ritual. For example, as noted earlier, Q 3:97 insists that "pilgrimage to the House is a duty to God"; Q 2:158 mentions al-Safa and al-Marwa; and Q 22:29 tells the believers to "go around the ancient House," meaning the circumambulation of the Ka'ba. The full elaboration of the ritual must be drawn from additional sources, like hadith and books that codify legal decisions and reasoning.

Muslims visit Mecca throughout the year, not only during the specified days of the final month of the Islamic calendar. They perform a shortened version of the pilgrimage ritual known as the *umra* in Arabic. Some pilgrims even precede their hajj with an umra. Non-Muslims may not enter the two holy cities of Mecca and Medina, a prohibition that goes back to the first centuries of Islam.

How important is charity and generosity to others?

Muhammad's early preaching repeatedly urged care and compassion for those less fortunate, and the Qur'an contains frequent exhortations to take care of the marginal members of society—the poor, the widowed, the orphaned. From these imperatives derive a central duty for Muslims, one of the five pillars of Islamic practice: *zakat* ("almsgiving" in English), the obligatory generosity to others that is closely linked to divine worship: "Righteousness that you turn your faces to the east and the west; but righteous is he who believes in God and the last day and the angels and the scripture and the prophets; and gives his wealth, for love of Him, to kin and to orphans and the needy and the wayfarer and to those who ask, and to set slaves free" (Q 2:177). The Arabic word itself carries connotations of purity and purification, so the generous gift of one's resources to those in need purifies both the donor and the donor's property. Many qur'anic passages connect zakat to required daily prayer, reinforcing the prominence of both practices as central to Muslim religious identity.

Zakat is an annual duty to God, and both the amount to be paid and the recipients are defined by Islamic law. The notion that *zakat* is an obligation to God, even before it is a responsibility to the poor, rests on the concept that what we possess, what we acquire, is not really ours but a gift from God. Giving to those in need simply returns to God what is ultimately his.

Zakat is calculated at a general rate of 2.5 percent on all personal wealth in excess of a stipulated minimum. Wealth includes income, real estate, cash, savings accounts, jewelry, and so on. According to the Qur'an, "The alms are only for the poor and the needy, and those who collect them, and those whose hearts are to be reconciled, and to free the captives and the debtors, and for the cause of God, and (for) the wayfarer"

(Q 9:60). Much interpretive ink has been expended defining each of these categories more precisely.

Zakat is properly given during the two major festivals of the Islamic year, 'Id al-Fitr, which marks the end of Ramadan, the month of fasting, and 'Id al-Adha, which occurs during the hajj season. These annual gifts connect the recipient to the larger Muslim community and reinforce the believer's commitment to religious brotherhood.

In addition to the religious obligation of zakat, other forms of charitable giving have deep roots in the Islamic tradition. Endowments to support educational institutions and public services have been a feature of Islamic culture since earliest times. For example, a visitor to major cities in the Middle East will often come upon public drinking fountains built and endowed centuries ago. The Shi'i form of zakat, known has *khums*, is distinguished by the requirement that it must be paid to the proper religious authority. These are the current representatives of the living, but hidden, imam, and they are charged with ensuring that donations reach their appropriate recipients.

American Muslims make their *zakat* payments to Islamic charitable organizations that have been established as registered nonprofits. Several of these with an online presence include handy *zakat* calculators as part of their websites. Others donate through their mosques or Islamic centers. Many direct their charitable giving to local needs, while others also send support to the impoverished in countries with which they maintain family connections.

8

FAMILY, SOCIAL, AND RELIGIOUS RELATIONS

What does the Qur'an say about love and marriage? About children?

The Qur'an's teaching about love starts with God. God initiates love in humans so that they can respond and reciprocate. When God is reassuring Moses about times that he has intervened on Moses's behalf, God says, "And I endowed you with love from Me that might be trained according to My will" (Q 20:39). It is from this divinely initiated love that humans are able to extend compassion and affection to others. It all begins with God and it all operates within the realm of shared faith in God.

Marital love is an extension of the transfer of love from God to humans. Although the Qur'an devotes far more attention to the legal and social aspects of marriage, some verses give glimpses of attraction and desire. Q 28:25–26 captures the courtship scene in Midian between Moses and the daughter of Jethro. Q 33:37 ("and you did hide in your mind what God was to bring to light") offers an allusion to the Prophet's desire for his eventual wife, Zaynab. Q 2:187 speaks of the marital bond with an unpretentious but touching metaphor, "They are garments for you and you are garments for them."

Marriage itself serves several functions. First of all, it makes sexual relations licit. Outside of marriage, sex is completely forbidden in Islam. Marriage also controls relationships within the community since certain unions are permitted and others are prohibited. A legitimate Muslim marriage begins with the prospective husband (or his delegate) approaching the father or guardian of his future wife. The contract itself, made between the man and wife, becomes legally effective with consummation and includes a dowry that goes to the wife. Muslim men may have four wives simultaneously—Q 4:3 is the Qur'anic warrant for this—with the proviso that all be treated equally. That condition has prompted some modern Muslim scholars to insist that the four-wife option is annulled by another verse, Q 4:129, which states, "You will not be able to deal equally between (your) wives, however much you wish (to do so)."

Divorce is a male prerogative. While the Qur'an urges the "firm bond" of lifelong love, it allows for the dissolution of a marriage when marital harmony disappears. Q 4:3, however, urges arbitration as a path to marital reconciliation: "And if you fear a breach between the two (the man and wife), appoint an arbiter from his people and an arbiter from her people. If they desire amendment God will make them of one mind."

A man can divorce his wife in various ways. He can issue a declaration of unilateral divorce, but it only becomes final after his wife completes three consecutive menstrual cycles, a constraint to ensure that she is not pregnant. This unilateral declaration entails economic consequences since the husband thereby loses the dowry or bride wealth that his wife brought to the marriage. Her dowry actually offers the opening by which a woman can escape an unhappy marriage. If she renounces her right to its return, her husband may be willing to release her. Another form of divorce occurs when a man forswears sexual relations with his wife and sustains this abstinence for four consecutive months. An unsupported accusation of adultery or refusal to acknowledge a child's paternity offers yet another way in which divorce become irrevocable. While divorce options strongly favor the husband, certain protections are provided to the wife. If, during the waiting period of three menstrual cycles, a woman discovers that she is pregnant, the divorce does not become final until the birth of her child. For two years after, the span of breastfeeding, she and her child are entitled to full maintenance.

More fundamentally, children represent one of God's principal blessings. Adam and Eve "cried to God, their Lord, saying: 'If You give to us a righteous child we shall be of the thankful'" (Q 7:189). Q 17:72 enumerates the divine blessings of family: "And God has given you wives of your own kind, and has given you, from your wives, sons and grandsons, and has made provision of good things for you."

Just as wives belong to their husbands, children belong to their biological fathers, and this Qur'anic injunction has far-reaching consequences in the custody laws of many Muslim countries. Another divergence from the legal norms of many nations is the prohibition on adoption. Although a number of Qur'anic passages urge care and concern for orphans, formal adoption is forbidden (Q 33:4–5). Breastfeeding also figures in the Qur'anic pronouncements about children, where the occasional need for non-maternal lactation is acknowledged. In Q 4:23, however, this counts as one of the prohibited marriage connections, that is, a man may not marry a woman who has nursed him or any females whom she has suckled.

An important problem is the continuing practice of child marriage. The custom persists, of course, not only in Muslim communities. It cuts across religions and cultures around the world. Countries with large Muslim populations and a high incidence of child marriage—defined as marriage before age eighteen—include Bangladesh, India, Mali, Niger, Sudan, and Somalia. But very high rates can also be found in Christian Nicaragua and Buddhist Nepal. Girls Not Brides, an umbrella organization that works to coordinate the efforts of many nongovernmental organizations (NGOs), maps the incidence of child marriage and tracks efforts at its eradication. In 2018, hundreds of religious leaders, UN officials, and child marriage activists gathered in Kuala Lumpur, Malaysia, to exchange information and ideas about how to combat this practice.

If a person dies, who inherits his or her property?

The Qur'an has quite a bit to say about bequests and inheritance and the later elaboration of these verses in Islamic legal literature has created one of the most dense and difficult subfields in the study of Islamic law. A saying attributed to Muhammad captures this complexity: "Learn the laws of inheritance and teach them to the people; for they are one-half of useful knowledge."

Not surprisingly, the relevant qur'anic verses about inheritance mandate a clear preference for family, both nuclear and extended, over non-kin. Also, the particulars of estate division operate within an underlying ethic of care and kindness: "To the men (of a family) belongs a share of what parents and near kindred leave, and to the women a share of what parents and near kindred leave, whether it be little or much—a legal share. And when relatives and orphans and the needy are present at the division (of the heritage), bestow on them from it and speak kindly to them" (Q 4:7–8).

While a person can bequeath property to specific individuals, several qur'anic verses regulate the shares of an inheritance that must go to particular family members. Required shares define the relationship of the deceased to his or her family members. A passage in Q 4:11, for example, accounts for varying circumstances: "to the male the equivalent of the portion of two females, and if there be more than two women, then theirs is two-thirds of the inheritance, and if there be one (only) then the half. And to each of his parents a sixth of the inheritance, if he has a son; and if he has no son and his parents are his heirs, then to his mother appertains the third; and if he has brothers, then to his mother appertains the sixth, after any legacy he may have bequeathed, or debt (has been paid)." This verse and the following one present basic provisions for inheritance and also clearly demonstrate the complexity of the topic.

A later passage, Q 4:176, sets forth additional and, in some sections, contradictory provisions. Much ink has been expended trying to reconcile these differences. Q 4:11 also expresses a feature of Islamic inheritance law that continues to generate considerable controversy, especially in our contemporary world. It is the statement "to the male the equivalent of the portion of two females." Some argue that since women could not inherit in pre-Islamic Arabia, this requirement improved their economic position. Others point to men's obligation to support their wives, children, mothers, sisters, and other female relatives, a religiously mandated responsibility that does not fall equally on women. Yet another argument contrasts this gender-based economic inequality with another, that is, the money and property that a man is expected to provide his wife as a marriage gift. But modern societies in which women work outside the home and in which international work opportunities take men far from the family members to whom they owe support would argue for a more equitable distribution of both financial obligations and inheritance shares.

Shi'i inheritance regulations, which differ somewhat from those of Sunni Muslims, place less emphasis on male relatives. Rather, they favor the nearest relations to the deceased, whether male or female. The favored group includes spouse and children as well as parents and siblings.

Is there a concept of community in the Qur'an?

While those of other faiths realize that they share their religious beliefs with people in different parts of the world, Muslims have a particularly strong sense of this. Key practices bind the Muslim community and continually reinforce the notion of global unity. The qur'anic term for this concept of a united religious group is *umma*, a word that occurs more than sixty times in the text and is ordinarily translated as "community." Q 2:213 speaks of the human race as originally united: "Mankind was one community, and God sent (to them) prophets as bearers of good tidings and as warners. . . ." Of the many groups into which this original unity splintered, Muslims are characterized as the "middle community" (Q 2:143), meaning a balanced society upon which others should model themselves.

A passage that has become famous as the "Verse of Righteousness" (Q 2:177) summarizes the essential qualities and attributes of this "balanced community":

It is not righteousness that you turn your faces to the east and the west; but righteous is he who believes in God and the last day and the angels and the scripture and the prophets; and gives his wealth, for love of Him, to kin and to orphans and the needy and the wayfarer and to those who ask, and to set slaves free; and observes proper worship and pays the poor-tax. And those who keep their treaty when they make one, and the patient in tribulation and adversity and time of stress. Such are they who are sincere. Such are the God-fearing.

This "Verse of Righteousness" clearly extends divinely mandated responsibilities well beyond family and tribal bonds. Such universality was also a key theme of Muhammad's preaching.

The idea of Muslims as constituting the "balanced community" or "the best community" is captured in the contrast that Q 3:110 makes with another religious grouping: "You are the best community that has been raised up for mankind. You enjoin right conduct and forbid indecency; and you believe in God. And if the People of the Book [commonly refers to Christians and Jews] had believed it would have been better for them. Some of them are believers; but most of them are transgressors."

Frequently, as in the preceding verse, Muslims are called "believers" or "those who submit," the literal meaning of the Arabic word *muslimun* (singular, *muslim*). Scholars have suggested that the first term, "believers," referred initially to all those within the early environment of Islam who shared a monotheistic belief and that only as the nascent Muslim community began to structure itself politically and economically did the designation shift to refer to that group primarily.

The Qur'an posits a primordial covenant between God and humans as a key factor in community formation. Q 7:172 offers the striking image of the first humans pledging their allegiance to God at the dawn of creation. Subsequent covenants, which God prescribes for his prophets and their followers, solidify this primordial act.

Does the Qur'an tell Muslims how to treat non-Muslims?

Within the last half-century, most major religions have given serious attention to inter-religious relations and interfaith dialogue. Countless meetings and conferences have been convened at the local, national, and international levels. Standing commissions and church agencies have been set up, all with the mandate to facilitate engagement of many sorts among people of different religious traditions. While some of these efforts and initiatives are bilateral (e.g., focused on Jewish-Christian relations or Hindu-Buddhist dialogue), many are multilateral, facilitating outreach to a variety of faith groups. Where does Islam, in all its internal diversity, fit into this panorama of inter-religious work? What are the resources from the Qur'an that foster or constrain Muslim engagement?

The Qur'an clearly reflects its origin within a multireligious environment. Although textual and archaeological evidence for specific religious communities within the Arabian Peninsula remains scant, the sheer number of qur'anic passages that evince an awareness of Jewish and Christian narrative and teaching—and, occasionally, of other religious traditions—confirms the prevailing religious diversity.

While some qur'anic mentions of Christians and Jews—collectively, the People of the Book—is descriptive, more of the text is focused on contrast, often critical. The Qur'an recognizes these predecessor scriptural traditions as stages in the sequence of divine revelation but judges them to be deficient. The message of Muhammad, God's final prophet, serves to correct the theological distortions and misrepresentations that have crept into previously pristine revelations. In short, the qur'anic attitude to earlier monotheistic traditions is supersessionist. Just as Christianity sees itself as superseding Judaism, Islam sees itself as superseding them both.

Traditional Muslim sources attest to encounters that Muhammad and his first followers had with both individuals and with groups who are identified as Christians. Generally these narratives serve a predictive or ratifying function. The Christians recognize the validity of Muhammad's prophetic vocation, or they acknowledge the congruence between his teaching and their own religious beliefs.

Two particular encounters have become enshrined in the history of Muslim-Christian relations. While certain qur'anic verses are connected to these experiences, both episodes receive much fuller treatment in the biographical literature about Muhammad. The first involves a group of the Prophet's followers who fled to the Christian kingdom of Abyssinia (what is now Ethiopia and Eritrea) to avoid persecution by the Meccan elite. Meccan envoys sought to recapture the emigrants, but the Christian Abyssinian king defended them when he realized how closely their religious beliefs resembled his own. The other involved the Christian community of Najran, an oasis city in south Arabia. While Q 85:4–9 has been understood as referring to an earlier persecution of Christians there, it is the biography of the Prophet that tells of a delegation from Najran that came to Medina and met with Muhammad a few years before his death.

The record of Muslim-Jewish relations, as drawn from the Qur'an and other early Islamic sources, is much harsher. Muhammad's expectations that the Jews of Medina would recognize him as a prophet of monotheism who testified to the same God as they did were soon dashed. Accusations of perfidy, treachery, and betrayal against Jewish groups in Medina resulted in banishment, enslavement, and death.

Can Muslims marry non-Muslims?

Qur'anic precepts on legitimate marriage partners do not display sexual symmetry. Men have much more latitude than women. Put simply, a Muslim woman may only marry a Muslim man. Muslim men, on the other hand, may marry "believing women." The governing verse, Q 5:5, states that lawful as marriage partners "are the virtuous women of the believers and the virtuous women of those who received the scripture before you." The phrase "those who received the scripture before you" refers to Jews and Christians, whom the Qur'an recognizes as recipients of the Hebrew Bible and New Testament, respectively. According to Q 2:221, however, Muslim men may not marry "idolatresses," those who do not acknowledge the oneness of God. In practice, this has often meant that Muslim-Hindu marriages present a problem. An additional phrase in Q 2:221, "until they believe," offers the solution. The prospective non-Muslim spouse must convert to Islam, a requirement not mandated for Jewish and Christian women who marry Muslim men.

Conversion, however, has continuing implications for the convert wife. Usually, she is expected to adopt a Muslim name, to give Muslim names to any future children, and to raise them in that faith. Adherence to other religious practices, customs, or symbols would be discouraged. The same expectations apply to Christian or Jewish men who convert to Islam to marry Muslim women.

In the contemporary world, the religious regulations and cultural expectations that govern interfaith marriage can differ markedly from the secular presuppositions of civil law codes. For most countries in Europe and North America, religious affiliation plays no role in a couple's eligibility for a marriage license and a civil ceremony. The state will recognize unions that religious officials may judge to be illicit. In Muslim-majority counties, where personal status laws tend to follow Islamic legal principles, there can be variation determined more by social and political factors than by strictly legal ones.

In Egypt, for example, while there are instances of Muslim men marrying Coptic Christian women, social pressures against such unions have become increasingly severe. The situation is not unlike that of Protestant and Catholic marriages in Northern Ireland, where social acceptance of such unions maps to the rise and fall of political tensions. To take another example, Jewish-Muslim marriages are quite rare in Israel since they must either be performed abroad and then registered with the state, or must involve conversion because marriage falls under the jurisdiction of religious communities.

Are there qur'anic passages about other religions?

The Qur'an identifies by name a number of other religions and expresses considerable knowledge of them. The traditional story of qur'anic origins points to a multireligious environment, and both archaeological and textual evidence, although limited, corroborates this. In the seventh century, a Christian presence on the periphery of the Arabian Peninsula can be traced in the monastic communities of Syria/Palestine and southern Iraq and in the tribal confederations that aligned themselves with the Byzantine and Persian empires. Syriac sources attest to the Christian community of Najran in southwestern Arabia, and a story in Muhammad's biography describes the encounters of some of the Prophet's followers with the Christian king of Ethiopia. Jewish communities in south

Arabia, and in other parts of the peninsula, have an even longer history, although the periods and patterns of migration and of conversion that created this presence are obscure. Both Muslim and non-Muslim sources speak of a sixth-century Jewish king, Yusuf Dhu Nuwas, who attacked Christian populations in retaliation for Christian aggression against his kingdom.

While the Qur'an speaks directly of Jews and Christians (both of which will be discussed later in this book), it also alludes to them, and to other groups, under more encompassing terms and categories. "People of the Book" appears dozens of times in the Qur'an as a reference to religious communities that came before Islam and that could claim reception of a revealed scripture. While the reference is chiefly to Christians and Jews (also called "Children of Israel"), later Islamic law allowed this to apply more broadly. Respect for prior scriptures found expression in the qur'anic injunction to consult their recipients: "And if you (Muḥammad) are in doubt concerning that which We reveal to you, then question those who read the scripture (that was) before you. The truth from your Lord has come to you. So do not be of the waverers" (Q 10:95).

Another category term, one with explicitly economic and legal consequences, is that of "protected person" or "protected people" (ahl al-dhimma in Arabic). Q 9:8–10 provides the qur'anic warrant for this terminology when it refers to the pact or covenant that Muslim communities can make with non-Muslims, offering them protection in exchange for certain kinds of taxation as well as some social restrictions. In mature Muslim societies of the medieval period, these covenants allowed minority religious groups to govern themselves and to practice their own rituals and liturgies. Although such social and economic disparities began to disappear with the rise of postcolonial nation-states in the Middle East and elsewhere, some elements of it remain. Iran, for example, recognizes only Jews, Christians, and Zoroastrians as legitimate groups and regularly persecutes Baha'is, while the Coptic Church in Egypt continues to adjudicate matters of family law. More recently, radical Islamist groups like ISIS have resurrected the concept of "protected people" as a way to coerce and control minority populations within their conquered territories.

According to most scholars, Zoroastrians are another religious group mentioned in the Qur'an but under the designation of "Magian" (*Majus* in Arabic). The term appears only once in the Qur'an (Q 22:17), where it is found along with Jews, Christians, idolaters, and the mysterious Sabians. Efforts to identify this last group have produced some interesting hypotheses but no definitive results.

PART III

EXPERIENCING BY SOUND, SIGHT, AND TOUCH

As God's words, the Qur'an guides Muslim belief and practice. It pushes the boundaries of life beyond the finitude of this world and orients the believer toward an eternal destiny. Its exhortations and admonitions mold the minds of youth, just as its promise of Paradise soothes the souls of the aged. But this sacred book affects more than individuals. It shapes and sustains entire cultures and manifests an enduring power that puzzles many secular Westerners.

Often I'm asked about this: Why is the Qur'an such a dominant text? How does it create and maintain its hold on the minds and hearts of Muslims? How do the words of the Qur'an reinforce demanding social and legal structures? Why do contemporary societies and their citizens give allegiance to a text that is almost 1,500 years old? Sometimes the tone of these questions is critical or even dismissive; sometimes it is one of amazement at the evidence of such abiding scriptural authority; sometimes it is fearful.

Part of the answer lies in the physicality of the Qur'an. For most Muslims, in most times and places, the Qur'an has been an aural experience, something they hear rather than something they read. The believer receives the divine words through ears and eyes, touches the text and traces its inscribed forms, tastes the elixirs of local healers. All of these actions provide ways of being immersed in the Qur'an bodily. The word writes itself on the body, shaping the senses, rooting its potency in flesh and bone. Memorization of the entire text—an achievement that can only be maintained by constant repetition—makes one a living repository of the divine word, a *hafiz* in Arabic. Accomplishing such a feat raises both the spiritual and social status of the hafiz and places him or her as a link in the chain of oral transmission that has carried the Qur'an from one generation to the next. In Muslim-majority countries, believers can hear the Qur'an throughout the day, not simply at religious services. Radio and television broadcasts, online videos, and smartphone apps allow uninterrupted access to professional recitation.

But while the aural experience of the Qur'an predominates, the visual is certainly not lacking. The eyes receive qur'anic words and verses in both textual and architectural forms. Colossal calligraphy adorns mosques, municipal structures, and mausoleums throughout the Muslim world. Such architectural embodiment allows the qur'anic word to define public and ritual space. The combination, in mosques and shrines, of communal chanting and monumental calligraphy creates for the devout an experience of verbal incarnation. The Qur'an also provides visual pleasure as a text, whether handwritten or printed. Major museums in many parts of the world own and display exquisite manuscripts of the Qur'an, some dating from the first centuries of Islam. With the production methods of modern printing, even mass-market copies of the Qur'an feature beautiful Arabic calligraphy, often with colorful ornamental embellishments.

Touching the text must be done reverently, with due regard for the purity regulations that govern ritual prayer and contact with the divine word. Tasting the text as a healing potion is more controversial, relegated by many religious leaders to the realm of unacceptable folk practice. Nevertheless, it endures in Muslim cultures around the world as yet another way to access the unique blessings of this powerful scripture.

9

RECITATION

How do Muslims study the Qur'an? What if they don't speak Arabic?

Turning a corner in downtown Dakar some years ago, I stumbled onto a sidewalk school. Clustered around a teacher under a small shade tree sat a group of young children with chalk boards in their hands. Carefully following the teacher's instructions, the little ones were trying to write letters of the Arabic alphabet on their boards. These Wolof-speaking children, like their counterparts around the Muslim world who are not native speakers of Arabic, were taking the first steps in their religious education. They would learn the Arabic alphabet and would then move to the rote recitation of some short verses and chapters (suras) of the Qur'an. These they would learn by heart, not necessarily understanding the exact meanings, but replicating the sounds and the rhythms under the patient guidance of their teacher.

Such elementary study sessions can be observed in all Muslim communities, whether in the formal setting of a mosque, madrasa (religious school), or community center, or in the less formal environment of teacher-student gatherings in village squares or city street corners. This time-honored system of students sitting at the feet of a teacher has ancient roots. It functioned for studying the Qur'an, but also for other educational endeavors. Memorizing was the primary mode of learning since books were scarce or nonexistent. Students might take notes, but mastery of a topic or a particular text depended on the ability to reproduce the teacher's reading and dictation by heart.

In addition to the study of Arabic and memorization of the Qur'an, the curricula of traditional schools included the sayings of the Prophet (hadith), some basics of Islamic law and theology, and rudimentary arithmetic. While such madrasas continue to exist, especially in non-Arabic-speaking countries like India, Pakistan, Malaysia, and Indonesia, they are no longer the most popular form of primary and secondary education.

As many Muslim-majority countries secured independence from the colonial governments that had ruled them for a century or more, educational reform became a pressing national concern. Parents, of course, want their children exposed to Islamic learning and Islamic values as early as possible, but they are also focused on preparing them for the modern economy and for contemporary occupations far more varied than that of religious leadership. To serve these two ends, modernized national school systems emerged, and many traditional schools expanded their curricula to meet demands for a more comprehensive educational system.

Such changes affected forms of higher education, as well. The training of religious professionals, whether mosque-leaders (*imams* in Arabic) or scholars (*ulama'* and *mujtahids*), has traditionally been concentrated in centers that have exercised intellectual leadership in the Muslim world for centuries, places like Al-Azhar University in Cairo, its Shi'i equivalents in Qom in Iran and Najaf in Iraq, or newer universities in Saudi Arabia, Malaysia, and Indonesia. All of these institutions can boast of international student bodies. For example, many students from Southeast Asia study in Saudi Arabia and Egypt, creating a continuous cross-fertilization of ideas across the Muslim world.

Muslims in Europe and North America have both repro-
duced traditional forms of Islamic learning and created new
ones. Mosques and community centers regularly hold Qur'an
classes for preschool and elementary school students after
school and on weekends. In European countries where religious schools are state-supported, Muslims have established
schools that, like Christian and Jewish ones, offer a mix of religious and regular subjects. Canada and the United States have
both seen the proliferation of private Muslim day schools at
the elementary and secondary levels. Although few in number,
there are even a few institutions that offer more advanced degrees or train students for work as prison, military, and hospital chaplains.

Why is the Qur'an always recited in Arabic?

In today's world, Arabic-speaking Muslims are a minority,
counting for less than one-fifth of the world's Muslim population. Yet most Muslims, whatever their native tongues, will
learn some Arabic, often at home, or in after-school lessons, or
in traditional Qur'an schools. Studying Arabic is an early step
in the religious initiation of Muslims. It's the gateway to God's
word, the Qur'an.

They will begin the study of Arabic with the firm belief that
Arabic is superior among all languages. That is why God chose
Arabic to reveal his final guidance to humankind. The Qur'an
itself talks about its language, identifying it as that of the
Prophet and his people. It names the language as "Arabic" (Q
26:195 and 46:12) and describes itself as "a Qur'ān in Arabic"
(Q 12:2) and "a decisive utterance in Arabic" (Q 13:37).

Later generations of scholars elaborated these estimations
about the superiority of the Arabic language and the unpar-
alleled excellence of the Qur'an's Arabic. They created a hierarchy of languages, including Hebrew, Syriac, and many others,
with Arabic at the summit. Arabic was Adam's language in the
Garden because God taught it to him. Although that original

linguistic unity was lost after the Flood with the dispersion of Noah's offspring, it will re-emerge in the Paradise of eternity, where we will all speak Arabic.

A corresponding belief judges the Qur'an itself to be in-imitable, unsurpassable in all respects, whether language, style, or content. A series of qur'anic verses have been interpreted as a challenge to any who think they could replicate this matchless scripture. Q 17:88 captures the thrust of these verses: "Say: 'Though mankind and the jinn should assemble to produce the like of this Qur'ān, they could not produce the like of it though they were helpers one of another.'"

Throughout their lives, whenever Muslims hear the Qur'an recited, whether in a mosque, on a car radio, or from a television screen, the recitation will be in Arabic. The words and meanings matter, of course, but equally important are the sounds and rhythms of the recitation. Its beauty and power have permeated Muslim lives for centuries. Hearing the Qur'an recited well can feel like being bathed in God's blessing. His very words resound in the mind and heart, giving the experience a sacramental quality, not unlike what reception of the Eucharist can be for Christians.

Many languages spoken by Muslims—Amharic, Bangla, Berber, Hausa, Indonesian, Malay, Persian, Swahili, Turkish, Urdu, Wolof—bear the imprint of qur'anic Arabic. Its words and phrases permeate daily speech from Marrakesh to Mindanao, providing a linguistic thread that weaves distant languages together. Some languages, such as Persian and Urdu, are written in the Arabic alphabet. The medieval spread of Islam into Europe affected language development there, as well, especially in Spain, Portugal, and Italy.

Do some people become famous for recitation?

The oral Qur'an is more important to Muslims than the written Qur'an. Observant Muslims recite passages of the Qur'an aloud as part of the daily prayer and for many, reciting longer sections or even the entire text is a pious practice. A belief in the unbroken, flawless transmission of the oral Qur'an from the time of its revelation to Muhammad until the present day gives the recited Qur'an final authority as the source of textual fidelity.

While young children in many, if not most, Muslim families learn some Arabic and memorize a few short sections of the Qur'an, some continue their study to achieve increasingly higher levels of accomplishment in memorization and recitation. Such study can be done in formal classes, in one-on-one sessions with an experienced teacher, or, increasingly, through the many self-paced audio and video tutorials on the Internet.

Correct recitation follows an elaborate system of rules that seeks to replicate the pronunciation of the Qur'an as the Prophet Muhammad received it. These rules establish its proper vocalization and determine its exact sounds and rhythms. Students start by learning precisely how to articulate the letters of the Arabic alphabet. Manuals for this instruction usually illustrate the places in the mouth and throat from which the sounds must be produced. Additional rules govern the assimilation and nasalization of certain vowels and consonants and the prolongation of particular vowel sounds. Places where one should pause or prostrate during recitation must also be practiced and learned.

The precision and complexity of these rules create two consequences: (1) it can take years to reach the most advanced levels of expertise in recitation, and (2) native speakers of Arabic do not have an automatic advantage. Anyone who learns to correctly replicate the required sounds can acquire a notable reputation for Qur'an recitation. In fact, some of the most famous contemporary reciters are from Southeast Asia, especially Indonesia. As the most populous Muslim nation, Indonesia has achieved a worldwide reputation for its recitation schools and competitions, as well as its nationally honored reciters, both male and female.

Reciters of the Qur'an who acquire an international reputation have, of course, memorized the entire Qur'an. But that
accomplishment is shared by millions of other Muslims. From
the very earliest periods of Islamic history, those who commit
the entire Qur'an to memory—who "preserve" the Qur'an
in their hearts—have held a special status within the community. Many Muslim families and communities mark this
achievement with a big celebration. Some seek an advanced
certification from those rare religious authorities who claim an
unbroken connection to the time of the Prophet himself. But
an impeccable recitation of the memorized Qur'an is not the
final event. Rather, it is the first step in a lifelong effort of re-
hearsal and retention. Like a concert pianist or a famous opera
singer, constant practice and repetition are mandatory, lest the
smallest part of the sacred text slip from memory.

Are there advanced degrees in qur'anic studies as there are in biblical studies?

Many are familiar with the years of learning required for the
preparation of Christian clergy and Jewish rabbis. We know
that some of these religious leaders continue their scripture
studies to an advanced degree, either at a seminary, a yeshiva,
or a university. Women and men who do not intend to work
in churches or temples or synagogues also do doctoral studies
in the Hebrew Bible and the New Testament in preparation
for academic positions and careers. These current forms of
scriptural study in Europe and North America build on the
centuries-long traditions of monastic education, forms of religious apprenticeship, informal networks of Bible classes and
schools, and various other methods and practices by which
Jewish and Christian scriptural learning has been passed from
one generation to another.

Islamic history shares a similar story of multiple modes of
knowledge transfer and professional preparation. From the
earliest period, a master-disciple model of tutorial instruction

introduced students to the fundamentals of qur'anic learning and to its memorization. Students who reached a high level of knowledge and recitation would be certified by their teachers as worthy links in a scholarly lineage that goes back centuries. The early period of Islamic history also saw the emergence of madrasas, schools of religious instruction that were originally connected with mosques and often offered boarding accommodations to students. Some madrasas added more advanced forms of instruction and they became the usual training ground for mosque functionaries and for preachers, teachers, and judges. Typically, students sat at the feet of their teachers and committed to memory the texts in which they were being instructed. If a student reached a high level of accuracy, he or she—some scholars in the classical period were women—could be certified to teach that text to others.

In the nineteenth century, as Muslim countries in the Middle East and elsewhere came under the influence of colonial powers, schools and universities based on European models began to replace or supplement the traditional forms of Islamic and qur'anic learning. Such universities are now the norm throughout the Muslim world, although traditional Qur'an schools and madrasas survive in parts of South and Southeast Asia and in some African countries.

At one point in my university teaching career, I had a chance to spend a semester at a major university in a Muslim country, the University of Jordan in Amman. My interest was more anthropological than academic. I wanted to sample a broad range of courses in qur'anic studies to see how these were taught to the emerging generation of young Muslim scholars. Just as if I had spent a semester at an American university following the curriculum of students who were preparing for PhDs in biblical studies, I experienced the breadth and complexity of disciplines that constitute the advanced study of the Qur'an. Here are the titles (translated from the Arabic) of some of the courses offered that semester: "An Introduction to Qur'anic Studies"; "Prescriptive [i.e., legal] Verses of the Qur'an"; "Recitation and

Memorization"; "Textual Study of Qur'an Commentaries"; "Principles of Qur'anic Exposition"; and "Hermeneutical Methods of the Commentators on the Qur'an."

But universities in Muslim countries are not the only pathway to PhD-level studies in the Qur'an. In the last three decades, increasing numbers of Muslim students now complete doctoral programs in Islamic studies at European and American universities with a focus on the Qur'an and its interpretation. Many have then been appointed to faculty positions in colleges and universities in North America and Europe.

10

RITUAL AND PRAYER

Is the Qur'an used in public worship? In other formal ceremonies?

Observant Muslims pray five times a day, a cycle of devotion they perform in private or in the public space of a mosque or other gathering area. Each of these prayer periods follows a prescribed set of words and actions, and many of the words are drawn from the Qur'an. For example, the first sura of the Qur'an, "The Opening," is recited multiple times during every one of the fivefold daily prayers.

The qur'anic references to the prayer cycle itself do not specify each and every detail. That is left to the manuals of hadith and the books of law that follow. Yet the Qur'an does refer to making the call to prayer (Q 5:58) and mentions some of the times of prayer, for example, "Establish worship at the going down of the sun until the dark of night, and (the recital of) the Qur'ān at dawn. (The recital of) the Qur'ān at dawn is ever witnessed" (Q 17:78). The five prayer periods also include the recitation of other parts of the Qur'an, which can be chosen by the worshipper.

Friday is the Muslim day for congregational prayer, like the Saturday Sabbath for Jews and Sunday for Christians. People gather at the mosque for the midday prayer, which is preceded by a sermon delivered by the leader, or imam, of the mosque.

The imam also selects those discretionary parts of the Qur'an that will be recited as part of the formal prayer. Some verses, such as the "Throne Verse" (Q 2:255) and the "Light Verse" (Q 24:35), are frequent choices.

The opening sura is also recited during other formal occasions, such as the sealing of contractual agreements, including marriage contracts. In fact, Qur'an recitation accompanies Muslims throughout the significant stages of their lives. Sometimes the nineteenth chapter, the sura of Mary, is recited to women during labor because it recounts Mary's sufferings as she gave birth to Jesus. In some communities, as young children begin to learn short sections of the Qur'an, particularly the first chapter and then the final section—the last thirtieth of the Qur'an with its brief chapters—their accomplishments are celebrated with gifts and parties. Graduations and other community events usually include recitation of the Qur'an.

Funerals can be the occasion for extended public recitation of the Qur'an. While verses may be recited during the preparation of the body and again at the gravesite, in some countries relatives of the deceased host a bereavement gathering after the burial. For example, in Egypt I have seen big events that involve the erection of a tent or the rental of a banquet hall to accommodate all the mourners. The central focus is a professional reciter of the Qur'an who is hired for the occasion. Mourners come and go, greeting the hosts and then sitting for a while to listen to the recitation and perhaps drink a small glass of tea.

Public Qur'an recitation is, of course, a feature of all major religious observances, such as the pilgrimage to Mecca, the commemoration of Abraham's willingness to sacrifice his son ('Id al-Adha), the end of the fasting during the month of Ramadan ('Id al-Fitra), and celebrations of the birthday of the Prophet.

What role does the Qur'an play in Islamic mysticism?

Mystical beliefs and practices in Islam, often grouped under the umbrella term of Sufism, resemble those in other religious traditions. Muslims who embrace such doctrines and devotions focus on finding a more intimate and individual experience of the divine, often through methods of meditation, world-renouncing asceticism, or particular prayer rituals. Such efforts developed early within the Islamic tradition, doubtless influenced by similar trends among religious groups encountered in Syria, Iraq, Iran, and elsewhere. Sufis grounded all aspects of their mystical endeavor in verses of the Qur'an and, over centuries, evolved traditions of qur'anic interpretation that stressed allegorical and esoteric readings.

They were drawn to passages that speak of God's being intimately present despite his all-encompassing majesty. A pair of verses in Q 20:7–8, for example, catches this contrast between divine omnipotence and intimacy: "To Him belongs whatever is in the heavens and whatever is in the earth, and whatever is between them, and whatever is beneath the sod / And if you speak aloud, then He knows the secret (thought) and (what is yet) more hidden." Another verse invites such approaches from the believer: "I answer the prayer of the suppliant when he cries to Me. So let them hear My call and let them trust in Me" (Q 2:186). The desire for divine/human intimacy is most famously supported by the verse (Q 50:16) that compares God's closeness to one's jugular vein.

As a spiritual practice, Sufism promotes the frequent recollection of God. Injunctions to "remember your Lord" (Q 18:24) and "remember God with much remembrance" (Q 33:41) stimulated the use of prayer formulas and mantras in both private and public devotions. Sometimes the public recitation of these prayer phrases incorporated physical movements, as well, such as whirling and circling in unison.

While the verses just noted invite and motivate the spiritual practices of Sufism, other passages bolster the conceptual framework that evolved from centuries of Sufi interpretation of the Qur'an. A particular focus was the famous "Light Verse," the name given to Q 24:35. The verse itself begins with the declaration that "God is the light of the heavens and the earth" and then develops the elaborate and beautiful simile of a lamp that glows from a blessed oil "though no fire touched it." In phrases that evoke the beginning of the Gospel of John, the verse continues with "Light upon light. God guides to His light whom He will."

Another passage favored by Sufi interpreters of the Qur'an places the connection between God and his creatures in a primordial context. Q 7:172 depicts a primeval scenario in which all future humanity is assembled before God in obedience and obeisance. As the totality of the human race, they testify to God's unsurpassed sovereignty over his whole creation. From this depiction grew a theology of the original covenant that God made with his creation in which each future human responds affirmatively to the divine question, "Am I not your Lord?"

A qur'anic term used to designate the developed ritual prayer practices of Sufi groups is *dhikr*, often translated as "remembrance." Q 7:205 conveys God's command to his Prophet: "And (O Muḥammad) remember your Lord within yourself humbly and with awe, below your breath, at morning and evening." Other qur'anic mentions of "the remembrance of God" (*dhikr Allāh* in Arabic) urge the repeated recollection of God's name, both by verbal expression and by interior contemplation. Sufi dhikr ceremonies in many parts of the world, including the United States, vary greatly but often include a litany of prayers, chants, and readings from the Qur'an that have been passed down from the founder of that particular Sufi community or order.

Can the Qur'an keep bad things from happening? Can it secure blessings?

For centuries, people all over the world have used scriptures and other important texts to find answers to pressing questions and to foretell the future. The method is simple: let the book fall open to a random page and whatever your finger or your eye first falls upon becomes the answer sought. The English word for this practice is "bibliomancy," and while some religious leaders condemn it as akin to witchcraft, others are more lenient. Seeking answers where the text falls open is but one of the popular uses to which the Qur'an is also put. While Muslim religious leaders reject most of these practices, they persist in all parts of the Muslim world.

Amulets, small ornaments that are worn or carried on the person, often encase qur'anic verses that are valued as an antidote to various illnesses or potential misfortunes. Holding the Qur'an's words close to one's body is thought to bring God's blessing (*baraka* in Arabic), and to reflect the Qur'an's own self-characterization as "a healing and a mercy for believers" (Q 17:82). The popularity of amulets gave rise to booklets that collected the verses considered most effective for healing, for protection against calamities, or for victory over one's opponents and enemies. Practitioners of religious healing, both male and female, operate in many parts of the Muslim world and are sought after for their knowledge of medical advice attributed to the Prophet and their ability to craft qur'anic remedies for many different situations.

Other uses of the Qur'an for healing, fertility, personal protection, or material abundance involve oral recitation. For example, a practitioner may recite the opening sura of the Qur'an (*al-Fatiha* in Arabic), and then blow or spit upon the afflicted person. People may do this for themselves, that is, repeat specific verses into their hands and then wipe the face and limbs to spread blessing over the body. Sometimes parts of the Qur'an are recited over water that a sick person then uses for washing or bathing. In another form of this, a healer will inscribe a particular verse on a piece of paper and then dip the paper in water to dissolve the ink. The ill person drinks the water to imbibe the healing properties of the qur'anic words. For example, Q 3:6, "He it is who fashions you in the wombs as pleases Him," may be used as a remedy against infertility and an inducement to conception.

While the practices described are widespread, even in the contemporary period, they are also regularly denounced by orthodox religious scholars who judge them to be nothing more than magic or sorcery, both of which are excoriated in the Qur'an. A centuries-long debate can be traced through Islamic religious literature about whether such traditional methods conform to the way of the Prophet Muhammad or fall well outside its bounds.

11

MANUSCRIPTS, PUBLIC ARCHITECTURE, AND MATERIAL CULTURE

How important is the Qur'an to art and architecture in the Muslim world?

Millions of people have made a pilgrimage to the Taj Mahal, waking at dawn to behold this white marble mausoleum as the sun's rays begin to make it glow. The Taj Mahal was built on the banks of the Yamuna River in Agra, a town southwest of Delhi, by a grieving husband, the Mughal emperor Shah Jahan (r. 1628–1658). Qur'anic inscriptions cover his wife's tomb, and also his own, as well as much of the interior and exterior of the building, providing a world-renowned example of the Qur'an as architectural embellishment.

Other famous examples abound, from the seventh-century Dome of the Rock in Jerusalem to such contemporary mosques as the Sheikh Zayed mosque in Abu Dhabi and the Hasan II mosque in Casablanca. Each of these showcases the splendid use of monumental qur'anic calligraphy. Eventually particular verses of the Qur'an became associated with specific uses. Mosque inscriptions often include Q 2:225, among the most famous verses, which begins, "God! There is no god except Him, the alive, the eternal. Neither slumber nor sleep overtakes Him. To Him belongs whatever is in the heavens and whatever is in the earth." Q 9:18 can also be frequently found: "He only shall tend God's sanctuaries [mosques] who believes in

God and the last day and observes proper worship and pays the poor-due and fears none except God."

Mosque lamps and prayer niches (*mihrab* in Arabic) often contain all or part of the famous Light Verse (Q 24:35), a verse that describes God as the light of the heavens, with a parable comparing his light to a glowing lamp within a niche lit with a luminous oil. Public fountains, a component of traditional urban life that were usually endowed by wealthy citizens, frequently feature qur'anic verses that count water as one of God's gifts to humankind or that speak of the waters of Paradise, for example, Q 76:17–18, "There are they watered with a cup whose mixture is of ginger (*zanjabil* in Arabic), / (The water of) a spring therein, named Salsabil."

In addition to being a source for apposite citations, the Qur'an shapes Islamic attitudes toward art in general, especially to the representation of living beings. It is often noted that calligraphy became a predominant art form in the Muslim world because of an aversion to figural painting and sculpture. While there is no direct prohibition of such artistic practice in the Qur'an, certain verses have been understood as arguments against it. References to "idols" or "statues" (Q 34:12–13, 6:74, and 5:90) became important elements of the more developed theological argument against the making of images. God alone is the creator, so there was strong opposition to anything, such as representations of humans or animals, that could foster idolatry.

Is there a tradition of calligraphy and illumination for the Qur'an?

A few years ago the Freer and Sackler Galleries of the Smithsonian Institution opened a landmark exhibit of Qur'an manuscripts. While some were from the museum's collection, most had been brought from the Museum of Turkish and Islamic Arts in Istanbul. It was the largest gathering of Qur'an manuscripts ever displayed in America and the exhibit attracted tens of thousands of visitors during its five months of display. Visitors marveled at monumental Qur'ans that had been commissioned by shahs and emirs. They peered closely at miniature volumes presented to queens and consorts. Every treasure in that exhibit demonstrated the artistic skill and pious devotion that had been lavished on these exquisite works of art.

Most major museums in the world count precious Qur'an manuscripts among their most prized possessions, and some have become especially noted for their collections: the Chester Beatty in Dublin, the Walters Art Gallery in Baltimore, and the Museum of Islamic Art at the Pergamon Museum in Berlin. One of the largest private collections has been assembled by Nasser David Khalili, a British-Iranian philanthropist, who frequently lends items to museums and galleries for display. His collection, and many others, have been digitized and put on the Internet, so it is now easy to view beautiful specimens from all over the world.

When arranged chronologically, such manuscripts reveal the evolution of a major Islamic art form, calligraphy. Because the Qur'an is understood to be God's own speech, writing or inscribing its words is both an artistic and a religious activity. From the earliest period, Qur'ans were written with great care, and over centuries ever more elaborate and majestic scripts evolved. The art of calligraphy required long training and skilled practitioners were prized, often finding patronage at royal courts.

In addition to employing elegant and embellished scripts, artists decorated Qur'ans for both aesthetic and functional purposes. These decorations were nonfigurative and nonrepresentational, respecting the religious disapproval of the representation of living beings. Functional ornamentation includes marking the end of each verse, noting divisions of the entire text into seven or thirty or sixty parts, and indicating where a person should bow or prostrate while reciting or listening to the recitation of the Qur'an. Such embellishment—frequently placed in the page margins—could be gold rosettes, or inscribed circles, decorative palmettes, or other features of abstract or floral design

Divisions between suras (i.e., chapter titles) often assumed more elaborate forms, such as the use of gold and other vibrant colors, as well as the insertion of demarcating lines to set off the title from the rest of the text. Some of the most magnificent manuscripts date from the late medieval period. These enormous productions can run to thousands of pages because each page carries only a few lines of text. The page itself may be framed with decorative lines and repeating ornamentation. Even earlier, fully decorated pages were found at the beginning and end of Qur'an manuscripts, especially framing its opening sura.

Are verses of the Qur'an ever written on ordinary objects?

Museums around the world attest to the popularity of writing qur'anic verses on objects both sacred and profane. Since the Qur'an is understood to be from God, its words are both a guidance and a blessing. Replicating those words with exquisite calligraphy on everything from architecture to amulets honors their source.

Coins were among the first objects to be inscribed with verses from the Qur'an. Before the end of the seventh century, gold dinars and silver dirhams were minted in Damascus during the reign of the Umayyad caliph, 'Abd al-Malik (r. 685–705). On their reverse, these coins carried Q 112:1–4, "Say: He is God, the one! / God, the eternally besought of all! / He begets not nor was begotten. / And there is none comparable to Him." Use of such an inscription signaled the caliph's religious and political loyalties and were a symbol of his power and legitimacy. The practice was continued by the Abbasid dynasty (750–1258) and by those that succeeded it. Later coins included different qur'anic citations and would often add reference to Muhammad as God's messenger, practices that continued well into the twentieth century. Q 9:33, for example, became a standard formula for thousands of coins: "He it is who has sent His messenger with the guidance and the religion of truth, that He may cause it to prevail over all religion, however much the idolaters may be averse."

Tombstones are another site of qur'anic inscriptions. An eighth-century tombstone from southern Syria counsels, "For the like of this (the rewards of Paradise), then, let the workers work" (Q 37:61). Q 3:185 is inscribed on a Tunisian tombstone dated to 883: "Every soul will taste of death." A somewhat later one from Mosul bears witness to the Qur'an itself as the uncreated speech of God.

The verses selected were usually consistent with the use intended for the inscribed object. A particularly famous instance of this is the Cairo nilometer. Nilometers were devices (e.g., vertical columns, deep wells, or descending steps) used to measure the height of the Nile River, whose annual inundation of its flood plain was crucial to Egypt's food supply. When the Abbasid caliph al-Mutawakkil (r. 847–861) ordered an early nilometer rebuilt, he commissioned the inscription of qur'anic verses on its interior sides. The verses selected emphasize God's benevolence in sending rain to nourish vegetation and sustain life. Q 50:9 is one of the verses: "And We send down from the sky blessed water whereby We give growth to gardens and the grain of crops."

Many others items of daily use, such as metal bowls used for medicinal purposes, plates and jugs used as tableware, glass lamps used in mosques and other buildings, and seals and amulets for personal use carry pertinent inscriptions and thereby elevate these objects beyond the ordinary and solicit blessings upon those who use them. Overall, the use of qur'anic phrases enhances any item that they adorn. They give it additional prestige and consequence, and they attest to the religious piety of the individual who created or commissioned the object, as well as to that of those who now own it.

PART IV

INTERPRETATION, INFLUENCE, AND GLOBAL DIFFUSION

The intellectual afterlife of the Qur'an—all the ways in which it has been proclaimed, interpreted, and promulgated since its first appearance—begins with the bedrock confidence that today's text is precisely what issued from the mouth of Muhammad, and thus from God. The related belief in the Prophet's sinlessness assures Muslims that his proclamation of the divine message was uncontaminated by personal corruption. The sinless messenger provides a secure foundation for a textual transmission that has been, and continues to be, flawless.

Like all significant works of scripture, the Qur'an has generated a vast and centuries-long enterprise of interpretation and commentary, one that evolved into a major intellectual endeavor and stimulated the production of an enormous literature. For well over a thousand years, people have spent lifetimes trying to understand and to explain every word, phrase, and verse of the text. Differences of interpretation have proliferated, fueling sectarian controversies among Muslims. Yet the centripetal force of the Arabic Qur'an binds the Muslim world together, despite such discord.

Interest in the Qur'an has not been confined to Muslim scholars. As Islam spread across countries and continents, awareness of this scripture and its adherents reached new audiences, stimulating both study and translation. The medieval effort by European scholars to translate and study the text in order to refute it—a motive that has never entirely disappeared—eventually evolved into a more academic interest, especially among non-Muslim scholars who had already immersed themselves in the post-Enlightenment methods of biblical studies.

As Islam's expansion built an ever-wider belt around the regions north and south of the Equator, its intellectual life flourished and stimulated the growth of educational methods and institutions. Matters of faith and practice engaged the best minds of the classical period, some of whom drew upon the Arabic translations of Greek philosophy as stimulants for both theological and philosophical speculation. Qur'anic citations anchored these enterprises, just as it shaped the creation of Islamic law and the development of defined schools of legal reasoning and jurisprudence.

Periods of forced exile and migration throughout history have created diaspora populations in all regions of the world. North America now has a significant—and diverse—Muslim community that, according to the projections of a prominent research center, will make Islam the second-largest religion in the United States by 2040. Islam is now an American religion, and the Qur'an is an American scripture. A rapid increase in translations of the Qur'an and related publications underscore this demographic reality.

12

INTERPRETATION

Can the Qur'an be interpreted?

Like any scripture or serious literary work, the Qur'an has been studied and discussed since its first appearance. According to traditional accounts, those to whom Muhammad first recited the revelations that he was receiving would ask him for explanations. "What do this word mean?" "Is that verse talking about something that actually happened, a historical event?" "To whom does that command apply, to everyone in every place or only to certain people and situations?" Rudimentary responses to questions of this sort can be found in the Qur'an itself, but more expansive explanations form the basis for a vast commentary literature that flourished over the following centuries.

As the Qur'an's message spread well beyond the Arabian Peninsula, it reached recipients who neither spoke Arabic nor shared the social and cultural background of those first listeners of the Qur'an. This contact spurred two developments: translation and more extended interpretation. Since all translation is itself an interpretive act, the earliest renderings of the Qur'an into neighboring languages, particularly Persian, involved interpretive choices. Equally pressing were the questions of context; new audiences needed to understand both the background and the applicability of specific qur'anic passages.

As explanations multiplied exponentially, early scholars sought to corral the burgeoning discipline of qur'anic interpretation with some principles and priorities. Eventually, a hierarchy of interpretations emerged. The best explanations were those that the Qur'an provided for itself. Scholars looked carefully through the entire text to discern whether one passage was amplified or clarified by another. Here is an example: the very first sura of the Qur'an contains the phrase "Master (or Owner) of the Day of Judgment." But what does that mean? Q 82:18–19 provides the answer: "Again, what will convey to you what the day of judgment is! / A day on which no soul has power at all for any (other) soul. The (absolute) command on that day is God's."

When no sufficient explanation could be found in the Qur'an, the next step was to search the words and actions of the Prophet as found in the hadith and other traditional sources. While there is no complete commentary on the Qur'an attributed to Muhammad, there are many explanatory comments to be culled from classical sources. In the absence of the Prophet's words, one could look to explanations provided by his earliest followers, the Companions, and finally to the statements of the following generation. For example, a frequently cited Companion is 'Abdullah ibn al-'Abbas (d. 687), the son of Muhammad's paternal uncle and a man revered for his knowledge of the Qur'an.

These initial explanations were often no more than simple glosses or annotations. Or they were brief descriptions of the setting or context to which a particular verse was addressed. Efforts to collate and systematize this disparate material resulted in the production of the earliest, often partial, commentaries. It was not long, however, before works were written that commented on each verse of the Qur'an in succession. In their fully developed form, these became known as "linked commentaries," and today they are often printed with the qur'anic verse along the top of the page and the paragraphs of interpretation below it.

Commentary on the Qur'an is a conservative tradition. Accounts from the earliest period record the voices of those who thought that any attempt to explain or interpret "God's words" verged on blasphemy. But the faith-seeking scholarly mind could not be stilled. As early as the ninth century, commentaries were created that covered the entire Qur'an. Over the next several centuries the genre expanded until the work of a single scholar could run to dozens of volumes. Part of the growth was the cumulative impulse. Later works included the interpretations of earlier authorities while adding the thoughts and insights of this latest author.

Commentaries on the Qur'an have been penned in every major language spoken by Muslims, and in their totality they present a formidable bulwark of religious scholarship, centuries long, deeply traditional—but still vital. Walking into bookstores in Beirut, Riyadh, and Jakarta, I have found tenth-, eleventh-, and twelfth-century commentaries that are still reprinted every few years and that continue to find new generations of readers.

From the earliest centuries of Islamic history, Muslim scholars have combined this production of multivolume commentaries with efforts to analyze and to classify the qur'anic text. For example, certain verses are labeled "clear," while others are consigned to the category of "ambiguous." Some verses are considered to be of general applicability, while others are understood to apply only to specific circumstances. Building category upon category, medieval Muslim scholars developed a highly sophisticated form of structural analysis that focused attention on an almost microscopic examination of the text, an effort and an attitude that further fortify the aura of unassailable textual authority that surrounds this scripture.

It would be wrong to consider such work nothing but an intellectual exercise. As with their monastic and rabbinic models, Muslim study of the Qur'an is infused with a sense of fervor and piety, of devotional response to the cognitive and aesthetic dimensions of the scripture. The mind joins the heart to create modes of scholarship that powerfully sustain a vision of the Qur'an as intellectually challenging and spiritually transforming.

What are hadith and are they part of the Qur'an?

How do we know what Muhammad was like and how he lived his life? This question is important to Muslims not simply for historical reasons, but because the Prophet is believed to be the most perfect embodiment of God's will. The primary sources for the life of Muhammad are known as the hadith. (In English the term "hadith" is used as both a singular and a collective noun.) The hadith record what Muhammad said and what he did during his lifetime. As a testimony to the way of living that he practiced and preached, they are a precious font of guidance for Muslims and a principal basis for Muslim law. Hadith also convey the words and actions of some of Muhammad's closest disciples and a record of events that occurred during their lifetimes.

Each hadith has two parts, a prefatory chain of names and then the matter being conveyed. Here is an example: "Yahya ibn Bukayr related to us: al-Layth related to us, on the authority of 'Uqayl, on the authority of Ibn Shihab [who said]: Abu Salama ibn 'Abd al-Rahman related to me: I heard Jabir ibn 'Abdullah [say] that he heard the Apostle of God [Muhammad] say: 'When the Quraysh accused me of lying, I remained [praying] in the enclosure of the Ka'ba. Thereupon God displayed Jerusalem before me, and I began describing it to them while I was still looking at it'."

The names are important because they provide the living links from the days of Muhammad through the generations that followed, right up until the time when that particular hadith was fixed in a permanent collection. It's the integrity of these transmitters that guarantee the authenticity of the account itself. To assess their reliability, an entire field of study emerged that compiled the biographies of those named in the chains of transmission and passed judgment on their relative reliability. It also examined the chronological sequence of the list of transmitters, assuring that their lifetimes had indeed overlapped. Medieval Muslim scholars were quite alert to the possibility of false hadith, pious forgeries that could ratify current customs with the unimpeachable authority of the Prophet.

These reports of the activities of the Prophet and his followers, which numbered in the thousands, were eventually compiled into massive collections of hadith whose current printed editions run to dozens of volumes. Such collections, both Sunni and Shi'i, remain a central repository of Muslim thought and practice. They stand alongside the Qur'an as a permanent source of religious guidance. The earliest of these collections was arranged by the names of those disciples and companions of Muhammad, including his wives, who were the original authors of the report. Later collections adopted a subject-matter ordering, with chapters on such religious topics as prayer, fasting, and pilgrimage, as well as subjects like commercial transactions, criminal punishments, and proper forms of dress and deportment. Shi'i collections emphasized the sayings of the Shi'i imams, starting with the first imam, 'Ali ibn Abi Talib.

The collections of hadith usually include an entire section devoted to statements of the Prophet that explain verses of the Qur'an. Such sections in the major collections of Sunni hadith, known as "The Six Books," touch upon a range of qur'anic issues, including the value of its recitation, the situations ("occasions of revelation") that specific verses address, elaboration of theological, ethical, and legislative interpretation, and the special benefits that accrue to the recitation of certain suras and verses.

Do certain verses in the Qur'an guide its interpretation?

In their efforts to gain ever-deeper insight into the Qur'an, generations of early scholars sought guidance in the text itself, in passages that suggested ways of understanding and interpretation. For example, Q 2:106 speaks about the idea of one verse replacing or "abrogating" the prescriptive power of an earlier verse: "Such of Our revelations as We abrogate or cause to be forgotten, we bring (in place) one better or the like of it. Do you not know that God is able to do all things?" This verse links to a concept of qur'anic chronology, a belief that the Qur'an appeared in stages and that it was possible to distinguish verses that the Prophet proclaimed later in his career from those that he conveyed earlier. The classic example of this concerns wine and other intoxicants. Commentators charted their progressive prohibition, beginning with verses that speak of their positive benefits (Q 16:67) and concluding with those that completely forbid any form of alcohol or mind-altering substance (Q 4:43 and 5:90–91).

For Muslims, the Qur'an is utterly unlike any other book. Not only does it encompass God's final revelation to humankind, but its language and its message are matchless. It is, in short, a miracle. Five verses in particular (Q 2:23–24; 10:38; 11:13; 17:88; 52:33–34) undergird this doctrine. Taken together, they are known as the "Challenge Verses" because they replicate dares that Muhammad issued to his opponents, defying them to produce anything that could equal the Qur'an. Here is one of the Challenge Verses: "Say: 'Though mankind and the jinn should assemble to produce the like of this Qur'ān, they could not produce the like of it though they were helpers one of another'"(Q 17:88). With the emergence of this belief in the Qur'an as a miracle, in its inimitability, books were written to describe and catalogue all the aspects of qur'anic rhetoric that demonstrate its utter superiority, and this topic became an important element of qur'anic studies.

A verse with potentially broad application, Q 3:7, begins: "He it is who has revealed to you (Muḥammad) the scripture in which are clear revelations—They are the substance of the book—and others (which are) allegorical." Like other sacred texts, some verses of the Qur'an can be read literally, while others should be appreciated as metaphorical expressions. Of course, deciding to which category a particular verse belonged became a matter of much scholarly debate.

Interpretation of the Qur'an drew from other sources, as well, such as information about the life of Muhammad and that of the early Muslim community. Trying to determine the historical circumstances to which a particular passage was addressed depends on a belief in targeted revelation. In other words, the Prophet received the Qur'an intermittently over the more than two decades that he was leading the emergent Muslim community. Issues would arise, and in prayer Muhammad would seek guidance from God about the specific situation. Later commentators would then draw a connection between a verse and the circumstances that prompted its revelation.

Are there different schools of interpretation among Sunni Muslims? Among Shi'i Muslims?

In many Muslim countries, a standard Arabic textbook for graduate programs in qur'anic studies divides the field of its interpretation into four sections. To set the stage for these divisions, the author first sketches the chronology of Qur'an commentary in three consecutive stages. The first stage is that which developed during the lifetime of the Prophet Muhammad and his closest Companions. The second covers the decades of those who succeeded those Companions as the spiritual and intellectual leaders of the early community. Stage three, however, is huge. It covers the many subsequent centuries of full-scale commentaries that produced the famous works that are still used and cited today.

It is this third stage that witnessed the development of different schools of interpretation. The textbook categorizes these as Shi'i, dissenter (a very free translation of the Arabic term), philosophical, legal and scientific, and modern. Another standard text, this one from a famous Hungarian Jewish scholar,

Ignaz Goldziher (d. 1921), speaks rather of five "directions" or orientations: traditional, rationalist, mystical, sectarian (particularly Shi'i), and modern. A yet more basic division runs between those commentators who based their interpretations chiefly on the statements of the Prophet and his Companions (i.e., on hadith) and those who expand beyond this.

For example, Shi'i commentators highlight verses that they understand as proof that Muhammad designated his cousin and son-in-law, Ali ibn Abi Talib, as his legitimate successor. Some commentators argue for interpretations of particular qur'anic verses that buttress a philosophical stance or perspective. Others probe the Qur'an to find deeper, mystical meanings in its verses that can support certain spiritual understandings and practices. Yet others concentrate their attention on those passages of the Qur'an that have legal implications. While only a small proportion of the entire Qur'an carries pronouncements that form the foundation of Islamic law, these have been a persistent focus for centuries of commentary.

Within the modern and contemporary period, additional emphases have emerged. Taking seriously the rationalist and scientific spirit of the post-Enlightenment period, some commentators have argued that there can be no contradiction between the laws of nature and the statements of the Qur'an since God is the origin of both. Through this lens, miracles become metaphors and modern science governs the meaning of the text. Taking another tack, some nineteenth-century commentators, often those with a medical or scientific background, began to insist that the Qur'an anticipates and confirms the findings of modern science. A frequently cited instance points to those verses in the Qur'an that speak of the creation of human life. Q 23:12–14, for example, states: "We created man from a product of wet earth; / Then placed him as a drop (of seed) in a safe lodging; / Then We fashioned the drop a clot, then We fashioned the clot a little lump, then We fashioned the little lump bones, then clothed the bones with flesh, and then produced it as another creation. So blessed be God, the best of creators!" For practitioners of scientific interpretation, this passage perfectly predicts the discoveries of the modern science of embryology. Although this exegetical orientation has not found wide acceptance among educated Muslims, it continues to attract ardent adherents.

Who decides which interpretation is the right one?

While Islam has no single, monolithic source of authority, the intellectual and moral qualities of deep learning and personal rectitude have always earned respect. From its earliest years, the Muslim community has honored religious scholars whose lives embody core values. For example, in the transmission of hadith (the words and actions of the Prophet Muhammad and his Companions), the virtue and integrity of the individual who passed the account or statement from his (or, sometimes, her) generation to the next counts significantly toward its acceptance as true or questionable. Biographies of the thousands and thousands of transmitters, biographies that recounted their education and their piety, were compiled into extensive collections in the classical and medieval periods.

That same concern for probity and erudition marks the discipline of qur'anic interpretation. In the first few generations following the Prophet Muhammad, interpretive comments on the Qur'an focused chiefly on the explanation of unusual words or offered brief comments to clarify ambiguities. As these early interpretive efforts multiplied, however, the need for their collection emerged. By the early tenth century, a Persian scholar stepped up to the task and produced an exhaustive inventory of what he considered to be all the reliable traditions and interpretations for every verse of the Qur'an. That collection—which in a current printed edition runs to thirty volumes—set the standard for subsequent Sunni commentaries. In the centuries after this first comprehensive production, commentators would carry forward much of what it contained and add their own analyses and insights. Commentary on the Qur'an became an aggregated tradition, and authority rested in that accumulated wisdom.

Training in the work of predecessors was requisite for those who would embark upon a new commentary, so the conservative nature of the interpretive tradition was inevitable. Although there were different schools and tendencies of interpretation—Shi'i, Sufi, and mystical, legally oriented—the intellectual tradition sought consensus that remained within an acceptable range. Too much deviation beyond that range laid the commentator open to the charge of "innovation," an accusation verging on an allegation of heresy.

In more recent years, and with the emergence of modernist interpretations, authority has also become associated with venerable institutions, like Al-Azhar University in Cairo, the seminaries in Qom, Iran, and academic study centers for the Qur'an in Saudi Arabia.

The Internet has challenged these traditional forms of authorization. Now everyone with access to a computer can offer interpretive comments on the Qur'an, and websites from all over the world host qur'anic conversations. While this has not diminished the prestige of more traditional forms of interpretive influence, it has democratized discussions about the Qur'an and significantly widened the range of participants.

Can anyone interpret the Qur'an or do you have to be an expert?

From the earliest period, the Islamic tradition has been wary of unrestrained and unrestricted interpretation of the Qur'an. While there is nothing that stops anyone from offering views on its individual verses, such musings are usually ignored. Acknowledging the huge gulf between divine knowledge and human limitations, some pious individuals in the first Islamic centuries renounced any attempts at qur'anic interpretation for fear of wandering into error. They could point to a qur'anic condemnation to justify this reluctance. Among the evil deeds noted in Q 7:33 is to "tell concerning God what you know not."

Over time, however, efforts to understand and to interpret the Qur'an developed into a full scholarly discipline. Extensive preliminary study was expected of those who would embark upon it. An advanced knowledge of Arabic grammar, vocabulary, and rhetoric was an obvious prerequisite. But the Arabic of the Qur'an, at least many elements of it, was not easily understandable to those now separated by several centuries from the time and place of the Qur'an's proclamation. Beyond the linguistic requirements, the potential commentator must be thoroughly familiar with the actions and teachings of the Prophet Muhammad and his closest followers, particularly those that shed light on the Qur'an. Often these will elucidate the occasions with which specific verses are connected.

Interpreters must also be knowledgeable about the earlier prophets and other figures mentioned in the Qur'an; must understand those verses that convey God's commands and have ethical and legal implications; and must be thoroughly familiar with the entire bibliography of classical commentary. No scholar who seeks to write a new commentary can ignore the work of his or her predecessors. To be accepted, scholarly authority must be grounded in deep familiarity with the full exegetical tradition.

But knowledge is not enough; spiritual and moral qualities are important, too. Sound understanding, Muslims believe, can only proceed from a pious heart and a life of obedience to the will and guidance of God. According to many sayings and traditions from the classical period, a sinful life clouds the mind, making it impossible to discern the truth and to achieve clear insight into the meaning and direction provided by the Qur'an.

In the contemporary Muslim world, where a university degree is more accessible than ever, the intellectual authority conveyed by traditional forms of religious education has begun to wane. In 1990 a Syrian engineer, Mahmud Shahrur, published an influential book about the Qur'an that countered the legacy of traditional interpretations and suggested new ways of reading the Qur'an, more attuned to the perspectives of philosophical and scientific rationalism. While Shahrur has found eager readers and has continued to write influential works on the Qur'an and on Islamic thought more generally, he has also been the object of strong condemnation from conservative scholars.

The growth of the Internet and the proliferation of blogs and other forms of self-publishing have opened yet other venues for commentary on the Qur'an. Although not always formally identified as qur'anic exegesis, these sites attract dedicated followers and stimulate conversations across national and generational boundaries.

Are there modern and contemporary interpreters of the Qur'an?

The centuries-long production of Qur'an commentaries continues. While the classical tradition shapes and structures contemporary interpretation of the Qur'an, it does not control it. New directions and emphases have emerged, prompted by the historical, social, and economic challenges of the last two centuries. Colonialism across the Muslim world, population migrations, intellectual disruptions, and massive political upheaval have all made their mark. A "modernist" form of qur'anic interpretation sought to engage the many kinds of change with which Muslim societies were starting to grapple. One offshoot of this has been the attempt to find in the Qur'an a foreshadowing of modern scientific advances. Another has been more structured. It groups qur'anic verses by topic and creates a subject-ordered catalogue of qur'anic wisdom.

More influential, however, has been the work of commentators who use the contemporary interpretation of the Qur'an as an opportunity to address political and social change. Arguably the most famous of these figures, at least in the Western world, is Sayyid Qutb (d. 1966), an Egyptian author and educator who was imprisoned and eventually executed for participating in the plot to assassinate President Gamal

Abdel Nasser. He wrote a Qur'an commentary called *In the Shade of the Qur'an*, in which he severely criticized social and political behavior, whether by non-Muslims or Muslims, that contravened Islamic norms. A key feature of Qutb's criticism was the charge that such behavior was tantamount to a return to the pre-Islamic "age of ignorance." Those who acted this way could no longer rightly be called Muslims and were susceptible to the consequences, such as assassination, that apostates incur. Qutb had little patience with the elaborate tradition of classical and post-classical commentaries, but wanted to return to the pristine period of the Prophet's lifetime. He created a manifesto for a new political order or, more precisely, for a restoration of the divinely ordained social contract of the earliest Muslim society.

Another form of commentary that has emerged, particularly in the Euro-American context, pays particular attention to those verses of the Qur'an that treat the social and spiritual status of women. In the first decade of the twenty-first century, several female Muslim scholars who have PhDs in Islamic studies from American and European universities have taken up the task of woman-centered interpretation of the Qur'an. While they are willing to acknowledge and respect the intellectual weight of the commentary tradition, they are also prepared to challenge it and to argue for new understandings less encumbered by the cultural weight of patriarchy.

Such efforts rely on a "contextualist" approach to interpretation, meaning one that takes full account of the Qur'an's historical context in order to discern the true spirit and continuing relevance of its message. The author of a recent study of this approach contrasts it explicitly to "textualist" methodologies, those that base themselves on the literal meaning of the text either entirely or in large measure.

Recent publications chart the expanding scope of contemporary commentary. From Turkey to the Malay-Indonesian region, from western China to Bosnia and Herzegovina, from Egypt and Iran to the Urdu- and Swahili-speaking parts of the

Muslim world, interpretation and translation of the Qur'an continues to flourish. One interesting study describes the emergence in Germany of qur'anic scholarship that neither carries forward the legacy of German Orientalism nor simply repeats the classical Muslim tradition. Rather, second- and third-generation Germans, many of Turkish and Kurdish backgrounds, are producing interpretations and translations in a new voice.

13

SCHOLARSHIP

How have non-Muslims studied the Qur'an?

Non-Muslims have always taken an intense interest in the Qur'an, but their motivations for doing so have been mixed. Through at least the first ten centuries after the birth of Islam—and sometimes still today—the usual reasons for studying the Qur'an were to refute it and to disparage it. Medieval Christian scholars bent upon proving that Islam was a false and even diabolical religion searched the text for evidence of these assumptions. As Islam spread into Christian lands, such as with the Muslim conquest of Andalusia, the effort took a more scholarly, if still polemical, approach.

The abbot of Cluny, a Benedictine monastery in France, commissioned the first Latin translation of the Qur'an in the mid-twelfth century. With this translation, as well as with the translations of other Islamic sources, Peter the Venerable (d. 1156) sought to acquire accurate information about Islam but only so that he could repudiate this "heresy" more effectively. Nevertheless, this Latin translation served as the source of translations into other European languages in subsequent centuries.

In 1734, the British Orientalist George Sale published an English translation of the Qur'an that found wide distribution. To it he prefaced a "Preliminary Discourse," a lengthy synopsis of Islam's basic beliefs, its early history, and the major teachings of the Qur'an. For at least a century, Sale's preface served as the primary textbook for Islamic studies in the English-speaking world. President Thomas Jefferson's personal library included a copy of this book and it shows evidence that he read it.

By the nineteenth century, post-Enlightenment study of the Bible—its history, its languages and literary features, and its sources—stimulated similar scholarship on the Qur'an. Several pioneering studies focused on the chronology of the Qur'an's suras (chapters) and verses. Non-Muslim scholars of this period sought to treat the Qur'an like any other literary text, independent of Muslim beliefs and most Muslim scholarship.

In the twentieth century, qur'anic studies as conducted in European and American universities expanded from this historical and contextual focus to the text's literary and linguistic elements. Attention was paid to words in the Qur'an that came from other languages, and qur'anic Arabic itself was compared to the known dialects of seventh-century Arabia. The influence of Judaism and Christianity on the Qur'an created a competitive field of inquiry, with some scholars insisting that Jewish beliefs and ideas dominate the text and others arguing that the strongest influence was Christian. A lasting legacy of this research is our much more detailed knowledge of the interrelations among the three great monotheistic traditions.

The final decades of the twentieth century were marked by some startling studies that challenged the entire historical tradition about how, where, and when Islam and the Qur'an emerged. One controversial book shifts Islam's origin from western Arabia to southern Iraq. Another suggests that the subtext of the Qur'an can be found in the liturgical language of Syriac Christianity, supporting this hypothesis with some ingenious etymological arguments. While neither proposal has secured scholarly consensus, both have stimulated new and interesting scholarship.

Is the Qur'an ever studied as a literary rather than a religious text?

For centuries, Muslim scholars have written eloquently about the literary qualities of the Qur'an. Whole books have been devoted to its vocabulary, its use of literary devices, its rhetorical structures, its metaphors and similes. In every way possible, they have judged it to be beyond compare, utterly without peer. By the ninth century it became dogma that the Qur'an is inimitable and that no human being could produce anything like it. All such classical scholarship, however, was conducted within a religious and theological context, with the explicit acknowledgment that the Qur'an is God's word. It never treated the Qur'an solely as a work of human authorship.

In the nineteenth and twentieth centuries, with the development of Western-influenced educational institutions, particularly universities, new forms of scholarship began to emerge. Egyptian author Taha Hussein (d. 1973) called for the study of the Qur'an as a great work of world literature. While not denying its religious relevance, Hussein wanted to see the Qur'an recognized as a masterpiece of literary art and a worthy object of modern literary research. His call did not go unheeded, and some professors in the Arabic literature department at what is now the University of Cairo in Egypt undertook such research and analysis. While they did not deny the Qur'an's divine origins, these scholars were willing to ask questions about its historical background and about what its words would have meant to the ancient Arabs who first heard them. From there the text could be examined both structurally and semantically and its stylistic features related to its thematic elements.

Although this scholarship aroused no significant controversy or opposition among religious conservatives, expansions of these methods certainly did. A doctoral thesis written in the late 1940s was turned down and its author eventually dismissed from his university position because he questioned whether the stories of the various prophets in the Qur'an were historically true. More recently, another Egyptian scholar, Nasr Hamid Abu Zayd (d. 2010), who placed even more stress on the cultural contingency of some qur'anic pronouncements, was charged with heresy and branded an apostate. In 1995, a Cairo court took the dramatic step of nullifying his marriage on the grounds that, as an apostate, and thus no longer a Muslim, he could not remain married to a Muslim woman. Fearing possible execution, Abu Zayd and his wife fled to Europe, where he took a teaching position in the Netherlands.

Scholars in non-Muslim countries, particularly in Europe and America, have a longer history of treating the Qur'an as a major work of world literature, setting aside its status for the believer as divine revelation. Post-Enlightenment study of the Bible proposed methodologies that were transferred to the study of the Qur'an by non-Muslim scholars. Even Muslim academics, such as the French-Algerian intellectual Mohammed Arkoun (d. 2010), have drawn upon a range of contemporary disciplines, from anthropology to linguistics, as appropriate tools for the interpretation of the Qur'an. The Shi'i intellectual Abdollkarim Soroush brings a philosophically informed understanding to the questions of qur'anic origins. His statements about the role of Muhammad in the process of revelation come close to a concept of scriptural inspiration and have provoked strong rebuttals among clerics in his native Iran.

Is there a connection between the Qur'an and the Bible?

Anyone familiar with the Bible who gives even a cursory glance to the Qur'an will quickly come across recognizable names and stories. Clearly, the two scriptures are connected through at least some of their contents. But there are other ways of comparing them, as well.

An obvious one is chronology. The Qur'an is the last of the three monotheistic texts—the Hebrew Bible, the Christian New Testament, and the Muslim Qur'an—and it considers itself to be both the culmination and the replacement of all previous divine revelation. This judgment is not dissimilar to the Christian attitudes toward the Old Testament and the New Testament, where the latter is seen as the fulfillment of the former.

Another comparison can be made of the historical, linguistic, and physical characteristics of the three texts. By word count, the Qur'an is the shortest, with 77,449 words in the Arabic text. Statistics for an English translation of the Hebrew Bible put the count at 622,700 and for the New Testament, 184,600. Behind the size differences stand very dissimilar time frames. The history of the Bible's formation can be counted in millennia. The books that eventually comprised the Hebrew Bible underwent a long process of collection and codification during which ancient oral traditions passed through many forms of authorship and editing. While the period that produced the canonical New Testament was considerably shorter, it, too, took centuries. At least according to its traditional accounts, the history of the qur'anic text is much more abbreviated, about two decades of divine revelation and a few decades of collection and codification after Muhammad's death. Linguistic variety also plays a part in this comparison: the biblical languages of Hebrew, Aramaic, and Greek versus the single qur'anic language of Arabic.

But the most common basis of comparison concerns shared stories, personages, and teachings. Here are just a few of the narratives to be found in the Qur'an and the Bible, although not in identical tellings: the creation of the heavens and earth, Noah and the Flood, Abraham's near sacrifice of his son, Joseph and his brothers, Moses and the burning bush, the annunciation to Mary, and the birth of Jesus. To the biblical figures just mentioned can be added Adam and Eve, Saul and David, Pharaoh and the Queen of Sheba, Zechariah and John the Baptist, and many more. Both the Bible and the Qur'an depict a creator God who brought human life into existence, who guides and blesses his creation, and whose final judgment ushers in an after life in Heaven or Hell.

Often the stories and personages that are shared among the Hebrew Bible, the New Testament, and the Qur'an are presented in quite abbreviated fashion in the Qur'an. There are few sustained narratives—the longest being the twelfth sura, which is devoted entirely to the story of Joseph—and some stories appear again and again in different parts of the text. It seems clear that Muhammad was proclaiming the Qur'an to audiences already familiar with these accounts, or at least with versions of them.

Has the Bible been used to understand the Qur'an?

As just noted, he Qur'an and the Bible are deeply interconnected, both textually and theologically. The Qur'an refers to the Torah (*Tawrat* in Arabic) and the Gospel (*Injil* in Arabic) and places itself within a sequence of divine revelation that produced those two earlier scriptures. Characters and narratives that appear in the Hebrew Bible and the Christian New Testament figure prominently in the Qur'an. Names like Abraham, Moses, and Jesus occur frequently in the text and, as just mentioned, Muhammad's audiences must have had some awareness of these personalities and their stories. Often the qur'anic accounts are short and elliptical, obviously alluding to tales so well-known that full elaboration was unnecessary. Where questions arose, contact with local Jews and Christians could fill in the blanks. Some early converts to Islam from these religions also served as possible sources of information. With the passage of time and with Islam's geographical spread, that initial familiarity became diluted or lost, making the qur'anic references to this biblical material more difficult to understand and explain. Interpreters of the Qur'an then sought to fill this knowledge gap by culling information from an even broader range of informants. A body of literature emerged entitled "tales of the prophets" that explored the lives of individual prophets and connected their histories to the qur'anic passages in which they are featured.

Embellishment and elaboration expanded the initially spare story outlines, creating a prophetic prehistory that stretched from the world's creation to the birth of the prophet Muhammad. But narratives closely—or loosely—connected with the Bible did not restrict themselves to the prophetic lineage. Countless Jewish and Christian folk tales and other edifying fables found their way into oral and written commentary on the Qur'an. As the discipline of qur'anic interpretation developed, however, its scholars became more discriminating, and by the early fourteenth century, a prominent intellectual like Ahmad ibn Taymiyya (d. 1328) was willing to dismiss most of this narrative elaboration as at best of no benefit and at worst of serious disservice.

While popular preachers mixed Jewish and Christian stories with their qur'anic counterparts, Muslim theologians were pursuing another track. They were seeking an uneasy accommodation between those qur'anic statements that disparage previous scriptures and those that imply their predictive value. Some verses in the Qur'an (e.g., Q 2:75–79 and 5:13) accuse earlier scriptures (i.e., the Bible and the Gospels) of being inadvertently damaged in their transmission or deliberately corrupted. That would argue that they have no continuing validity and have been completely superseded or abrogated by the Qur'an. On the other hand, there are passages in the Qur'an (Q 2:127–129; 7:157; 61:6) that point back to the Hebrew Bible and the New Testament as foretelling Muhammad's eventual arrival. This motivated Muslim scholars to scour these scriptures for such predictive passages. An often-cited example is Deuteronomy 18:18, which is taken to be a clear anticipation of Muhammad: "I will raise up for them a prophet like you [Moses] from among their own people; I will put my words in the mouth of the prophet who shall speak to them everything that I command."

14

INFLUENCE

How did the Qur'an shape Islamic philosophy and theology?

The Qur'an's core message is that God is one, that he is both creator and judge, and that the text reveals his will and guidance for his creation. These themes reinforce earlier forms of theological monotheism as they developed in late antiquity. In this mature understanding of monotheism, God's omnipotence is universal, determining the fate of each individual as well as of the universe as a whole. He is no longer the god of a single people, but the lord of all. This fundamental conception is captured in one of the shortest suras: "Say: He is God, the one! / God, the eternally besought of all! / He begets not nor was begotten. / And there is none comparable to Him" (Q 112:1–4).

In the early centuries of Islam, scholars grappled with the implications of these basic beliefs. Why did God create the world and humankind? As creator of the universe, does God continue to care for his creation? If God is all-powerful, determining everything that happens, do humans have free will, or are all their actions predestined? What happens after death and how does God exercise his divine judgment? Does a Muslim who commits grave sin thereby cease to be a Muslim? Theology—or *kalam* in Arabic—developed as the systematic study of these questions and many others. Contact with

Christian theology and Greek philosophy expanded the range of issues and arguments. Divergent views and emphases created schools of thought, some of which aligned with the sectarian divisions of Sunni and Shi'i and others that crossed those boundaries. Nevertheless, in all of these schools and in the literature they produced, reference to the Qur'an (and the hadith) constitutes the irrefutable basis of every assertion.

The cultivation of philosophy, understood as the rational investigation of first principles and causes, entered the intellectual sphere of Islam largely through its contact with classical Greek thinkers and their successors. As a methodology based on the primacy of human reason, philosophical reflection on the Qur'an was not welcomed by many early Muslim scholars. How could rational discourse dare to engage the divine word? This contact also generated a series of questions that challenged fundamental qur'anic assertions. An instance of this would be qur'anic statements about the resurrection of the body, the physical delights of Paradise, and the corporeal torments of Hell, statements which few philosophers could accept as literal. Another concerns God's knowledge of "particulars." While the Qur'an depicts a God who is intimately involved with his creation and witnesses every action of his creatures, the Greek philosophical tradition insisted that God could only know universal principles but not the details of daily life.

An even more comprehensive conflict between philosophical and theological ways of knowing revolved around their relative value. Islamic philosophers asserted a gradation in ways of knowing, a calibration suited to particular classes of people. The masses could only understand religious language, while the enlightened were capable of grasping the more rarefied truths that philosophical reasoning could achieve.

Contemporary Muslim thinkers, both theologians and philosophers, continue to explore and expand these earlier lines of investigation. A form of mystical philosophy that flourished in sixteenth-century Persia and beyond remains an important influence on modern Sufi thought. Both modernist theologians and twentieth- and twenty-first-century political theorists have drawn upon the Qur'an to address situations and issues that could not have been predicted by their intellectual forebears.

What is the relationship between the Shari'a and the Qur'an?

As Arab-Islamic terms have entered the English vocabulary, few words have caused more confusion than "Shari'a." Hearing its use in the phrase "Shari'a law," many immediately assume that it's simply another legal system, like civil law or common law. They imagine libraries of bound volumes like those found in a lawyer's office or judge's chambers. And, of course, most will associate it with corporal punishments, like stoning for adultery and hand-chopping for theft. But the Shari'a is not a printed law code; it's an umbrella concept or a way of thinking about how God wants to govern human actions. Although the Shari'a has operated differently in different times and places, it has remained a coherent legal tradition and the object of intensive study and application by Muslim legal scholars and religious thinkers for the past fifteen centuries.

As understood and organized by these scholars, the Shari'a derives its fundamental precepts and principles from both the Qur'an and the *sunna*, the authoritative practice of the Prophet Muhammad as codified in the hadith. Methods of inferential reasoning allowed jurists to apply legal prescriptions drawn from these sources to new questions and situations, while the retrospective ratification of such applications, achieved through the consensus of a generation of jurists, built the foundation for the further expansion of legal reasoning. This centuries-long process of translating God's law, as enshrined in the Qur'an and the *sunna*, into actual, applicable human rules and regulations created the legal codes of the Muslim world.

Again, despite what some presume, the Qur'an contains relatively little material that could be considered unequivocally prescriptive. Most estimates place the number of verses with explicitly legal content at about 500 out of more than 6,000 verses overall. Nevertheless, the Qur'an positions itself within the scriptural traditions that mandate and legislate for their followers. A long passage in the fifth sura speaks of the earlier scriptures, the Torah and Gospel, as the law by which Jews and Christians, respectively, should judge and be judged. It turns, then, to the Muslim community with these words: "And to you have We revealed the scripture with the truth, confirming whatever scripture was before it, and a watcher over it. So judge between them by what God has revealed. . . . For each We have appointed a divine law and a traced-out way" (Q 5:48).

Not only does the Qur'an convey statements that regulate Muslim life, it also shows the gradual development of some of its mandates. The most famous instance of this is the regulation of alcohol. An early, positive mention of date-wine and grape-wine in a Meccan sura (Q 16:67) becomes modified in the Medinan period (Q 2:219 and 4:43) until the proclamation of a final, categorical prohibition in Q 5:90–91 that links alcohol with gambling and idol worship: "O you who believe! Strong drink and games of chance and idols and divining arrows are only an infamy of Satan's handiwork. Leave it aside in order that you may succeed."

As noted earlier, this example can open a discussion of another factor in the relation between Qur'an and Shari'a, the theory of abrogation. Two verses in the Qur'an (Q 2:106 and 16:101) assert that God can substitute a later, better revelation for an earlier one. The replacement nullifies the legislative force of the original verse. Medieval scholars wrote complicated and detailed treatises that define the theological and philosophical intricacies of this concept of abrogation as it operates within the Qur'an and between the Qur'an and *sunna*. Related to this concept of sequential nullification is the more comprehensive assertion that the revelation to Muhammad supersedes and abrogates previous scriptures (i.e., the Torah and the Gospel).

What is the connection between the Qur'an and contemporary science?

Muslim contributions to science in the medieval period proved critical for later Western scientific advances. Major Greek scientific and philosophical works, but also those written in Syriac, Sanskrit, and Persian languages, came into Latin via Arabic translation. The Abbasid caliph Al-Ma'mun (r. 813–833) built his House of Wisdom in Baghdad, making it a renowned library and a center for these translation activities, one that relied upon the efforts of Muslim, Christian, and Jewish scholars.

Such scholarly attention to scientific knowledge may have been encouraged by the Qur'an's exaltation of the created world and its urging humans to reflect on nature as signs of its creator. As an intellectual pursuit, however, scientific study and investigation were not tightly tied to the Qur'an itself. Rather, the connection was more general as, for example, when religious requirements necessitated certain studies, such as astronomical calculations to determine the exact orientation toward Mecca, the precise times for ritual prayer, and the onset of Ramadan, the month of fasting.

In contemporary Islamic discourse, however, the connection between science and the Qur'an has grown much closer. Countless books, articles, and conferences focus on how science can prove the divine nature of the Qur'an. "Islam as a religion of science" has become a byword for these initiatives. Only now, according to such thinkers, can we begin to understand the Qur'an's predictions of technological advances centuries before humans had even begun to contemplate them, far less achieve them. These allusions to the modern findings of science constitute, according to such thinkers, the miracle of the Qur'an. The soft form of this is the assertion that nothing in the Qur'an contradicts the findings of modern science. The most famous proponent of this view is the French physician Maurice Bucaille (d. 1998). His book, *The Bible, the Qur'an and Science: The Holy Scriptures Examined in the Light of Modern*

Knowledge (1976), has gone through multiple editions and has been translated into many languages.

While classical commentaries elaborated on natural phenomena, such as the movement of the stars and the succession of day and night, their purpose was to emphasize God's use of creation to maximize human benefit. It was not until the nineteenth and early twentieth centuries that Muslim interpreters of the Qur'an began to promote this explicitly "scientific exegesis." An instance of this, as promoted by Bucaille and others, would be claims that qur'anic references to the stages of human creation miraculously replicate the patterns of fetal development discovered by the modern science of embryology. Although this "scientific exegesis" has attracted a considerable number of followers, it has also drawn the attention of many critics, such as those who dismiss this line of inquiry as producing forced readings that limit the rich interpretive range of God's revelation. Nevertheless, publications that promote the predictive power of the Qur'an continue to be produced, such as the four-volume work by the Egyptian geologist Zaghlul al-Najjar, titled *A Commentary on the Cosmic Verses of the Qur'an.*

What role does the Qur'an play in Arabic literature? In the literatures of other Muslim cultures?

The Qur'an has exerted an enduring influence on every area of intellectual and artistic activity within the Muslim world. Understood to be the very word of God, the Qur'an has shaped not only human lives but also cultural environments, touching all subsequent stages of literary development in Arabic and many other languages. Qur'anic words and phrases have permeated every literary genre, and its themes, imagery, and metaphors have found their way into works intended for general and specialized audiences.

While classical literary historians attribute the Qur'an's influence to the beauty and grandeur of its language and composition, another element deserves attention. Until the last century, most Muslims—like most people everywhere—were illiterate. They did not read the Qur'an, but they heard it preached and recited. And many of them memorized all or much of the text, ingesting a mental repertoire of ideas and images that was always available. Phrases and passages from the Qur'an, often unidentified and sometimes rephrased, were incorporated into all forms of literary production.

Major qur'anic figures like Abraham, Moses, Joseph, and Pharaoh assume stock characterization in later prose and poetry based on their qur'anic depictions. Well-known prophet stories drawn from the Qur'an are refashioned as more extended and elaborated narratives, creating a whole subgenre of Islamic religious literature. The longest narrative in the Qur'an is sura 12, which tells the story of Joseph and his brothers and of Joseph's life in Egypt as a high official in Pharaoh's household. Many versions of this tale can be found in Arabic and other Islamic languages—even an Iranian miniseries.

As qur'anic influence moved into languages like Persian, Turkish, and Urdu, it enriched the vocabularies of these languages and expanded the storehouse of narrative material. Among the most famous works of medieval Persian literature is the *Conference of the Birds* by Farid al-Din Attar (d. 1230). This mystical poem draws directly on the qur'anic story of the prophet Solomon, who had been "taught the language of birds" (Q 27:16), and used the hoopoe bird as his guide and envoy.

Muhammad Iqbal (d. 1938), a renowned Urdu poet and the spiritual father of Pakistan, wrote a "Complaint" addressed to God. Full of qur'anic allusions, it demonstrates the enduring literary legacy of the Qur'an. A verse from the poem:

> We erased the smudge of falsehood from the parchment
>   firmament,
> We redeemed the human species from the chains of
>   slavery;
> And we filled the Holy Kaaba [central shrine in Mecca]
>   with our foreheads humbly bent,

Clutching to our fervent bosoms the Koran in ecstasy,
Yet the charge is laid against us that we have played the
     faithless part;
If disloyal we have proved, hast Thou deserved to win
     our heart? (From *The Complaint and Answers*, trans.
     A. J. Arberry.)

The eventual influence of Islamic literature, deeply infused with qur'anic language and themes, on Western literature— medieval troubadour poetry, Dante, Boccaccio, Chaucer, Cervantes, and more—remains a lively field of scholarly investigation.

15

TRANSLATION
AND TRANSMISSION

Are Muslims allowed to translate the Qur'an?

Translating the Qur'an presents Muslims with a theological problem. Most Jews and Christians read the Bible in their native languages and feel comfortable calling that "the Bible." They may realize that the original languages of the documents that now comprise the Hebrew Bible and the Christian Old and New Testaments are Hebrew, Greek, and Aramaic, but that does not give those languages a special status. For Muslims the situation is different. The Qur'an was revealed in Arabic (Q 12:2, "We have revealed it, a Qur'an in Arabic, that you may understand") and, at least initially, it was understood to be addressed chiefly to the Arabs. Other peoples had received revelations from God in their languages: "And We never sent a messenger except with the language of his people, that he might make (the message) clear for them" (Q 14:4). Now it was the turn of the Arabs: "Thus have We revealed it, a decisive utterance in Arabic" (Q 13:37).

But as Islam quickly spread beyond the Arabian Peninsula, especially in the decades following Muhammad's death, the question of how to convey God's final revelation to people who could not speak Arabic soon arose. Certainly, the meaning of the Qur'an could be paraphrased in popular preaching. That was not a problem. But efforts to actually translate the text into other languages immediately opened the question of what status those translations had. Could they be used in formal worship? Were public recitations of the Qur'an in translation as valid as in Arabic? The unequivocal answer has been "no." The Qur'an is only the Qur'an in Arabic. Since the Muslim understanding of revelation is closer to a doctrine of dictation than of divine inspiration, this makes perfect sense. Muhammad received God's very words in Arabic. They are collected and enshrined in the Qur'an and that gives the text—and the language in which it was revealed—a sacredness that surpasses all others.

Of course, translations and paraphrases were soon produced. An early example can be found in a Persian manuscript that presents each line of the Arabic text with an interlinear Persian translation written in a smaller script directly beneath it. The Persian translation hews closely to the Arabic in both syntax and word selection. While more modern translations, in Persian and other languages, allow themselves great latitude, they always recognize and acknowledge their subservience to the Arabic original. Formats may vary, with interlinear and facing-page being the most common, but publishing such translations along with the Arabic original remains the prevailing preference. In 1937, Al-Azhar University in Cairo, an ancient and prominent place of Islamic learning and an authoritative institution for Sunni Islam, issued an important decree. In a ruling later confirmed by the Egyptian Council of Ministers, Al-Azhar confirmed that Qur'an translations in other languages could not bear the simple title "Qur'an." Their titles must carry a phrase like "The Meaning of" or "The Interpretation of" the Qur'an in order to make clear that they are not to be considered the Qur'an itself.

Reinforcing the uniqueness of the Arabic Qur'an was the doctrine of the Qur'an's inimitability, the belief that no human effort could replicate its power and majesty or match its rhetorical transcendence. The doctrine of inimitability became a more prominent theological construct in the ninth century and, in its fully developed form, this doctrine supports claims for the eloquence of the entire Arabic language. The doctrine also emphasizes that the Qur'an is a miracle. In classical Islamic literature there are lists of all the ways in which the Qur'an cannot be matched or surpassed: its language is better than other languages; its style is better than other styles; its completeness has no equal; there is no contradiction between it and any human knowledge.

When was the Qur'an translated into European languages?

As the qur'anic message spread into Persia and Turkey, translations and commentaries in those languages began to appear, with a Persian translation of the famous Arabic commentary by Abu Ja'far ibn Jarir al-Tabari (d. 923) being among the first to be produced.

The first translations into European languages, however, were not motivated by religious need or cultural curiosity. Rather, they were initiated by those, chiefly Christian, who wished to confront and combat this new "heresy." The earliest full translations that survive are in Latin. The oldest of these dates to twelfth-century Spain and to the efforts of Peter the Venerable (d. 1156), the Abbot of Cluny, a monastic establishment in eastern France. At that time, Spain was split between Muslim and Christian kingdoms, and cultural contacts between these regions created a lively translation industry focused mainly on scientific and philosophical works.

On a trip to Spain, Abbot Peter commissioned an English scholar, Robert of Ketton, to produce a Latin version of the Qur'an. He accomplished this by 1143, and the title under which the translation subsequently circulated, *The Law of the Pseudoprophet Mohamet*, clearly demonstrates the motivation for its production. Ketton's paraphrase provided the basis for several other translations in the medieval period and was issued several centuries later by a bookseller in Basel and Zurich.

In the mid-sixteenth and mid-seventeenth centuries, Qur'an translations in Italian, German, and French appeared. The

French translation by André du Ryer was the basis for the first English-language translation by Alexander Ross. In 1734 the British Arabist George Sale published a translation of the Qur'an made directly from the Arabic, with the help of an earlier Latin rendering, and he prefaced it with a "Preliminary Discourse" that introduced readers to the life of Muhammad and the basic tenets of Islam. President Thomas Jefferson owned a copy of Sale's translation which, along with the rest of his library, he sold to the Library of Congress to create the foundation of its future collection. Representative Keith Ellison, the first Muslim elected to Congress, was sworn in on this copy.

In the twentieth and twenty-first centuries, English translations of the Qur'an have proliferated, with a particular surge after the horrific events of September 11, 2001. A recent bibliography listed more than sixty versions and new ones continue to appear. Among the most interesting is *The American Qur'an* by the contemporary artist Sandow Birk, a unique work that draws from several existing English translations, combining these with extraordinary illustrations of American life and of key moments in this country's recent history.

When was the Qur'an first printed?

A copy of the Gutenberg Bible remains on permanent display in the Great Hall of the Library of Congress. Dated to the mid-fifteenth century, extant copies of the Gutenberg Bible are revered not only for their religious value but also as markers that ushered in the age of book printing in the West.

European Christians learned the art of papermaking from the Muslims who ruled Spain in the medieval period. Paper mills in Germany provided the handmade sheets upon which Johann Gutenberg began printing books. Muslims, in turn, encountered the Chinese method of papermaking through their eighth-century conquest of Central Asia but, unlike in Europe, printing did not quickly follow the discovery of paper in the Islamic world. Almost a thousand years passed before book printing took hold in Muslim countries, with the first printing press established in Istanbul early in the eighteenth century. But one book that was not printed on that Ottoman press was the Qur'an.

Creating movable type to print Arabic is a complex operation. Arabic is a cursive script with joins between the letters and with the letters themselves using different forms depending on whether they fall at the beginning, middle, or end of a word. Vowel markings and other diacritics further complicate the typographical challenges. A complete font of Arabic type can include well over 600 "sorts" or font elements.

But alphabetic complexity was not the only issue. There was considerable resistance to printing generally and to the printing of the Qur'an, in particular. Part of it was economic— a huge industry of book copyists and calligraphers would find themselves jobless—and part of it was religious. How could a moving-type machine replicate the reverent care and spiritual attention with which a scribe forms each handwritten letter? Further, many religious scholars viewed the printing press as a harmful innovation and were repulsed at the thought of metal letters exerting pressure to push the word "God" onto paper. Others recognized that while human scribes could make themselves ritually pure before touching the text, a machine could itself be a source of contaminants and pollution. Finally, there was concern about quality control. Early printed Qur'ans, including a recently surfaced Venetian effort, were not error-free and thus provided the religious authorities with yet another reason to resent and resist this "new" technology.

Consequently, the first printed editions of the Qur'an were not produced in the Middle East but in Europe. Robert of Ketton's Latin translation had been printed several times by the middle of the sixteenth century. The first printed Arabic Qur'an was produced in Venice. This 1537–1538 production was thought to have completely vanished in flames until a lone copy was found in the 1980s in a Venetian monastery. After that, printed editions appeared in several European countries, like Germany and Russia. The nineteenth century witnessed a proliferation of printing in the Muslim world, from India to Iran and from Turkey to Egypt, and by the middle of the century there were locally printed Qur'ans in virtually every part of the Muslim world. The Bulaq Press, the first official government press in Egypt, played a particularly prominent role in this development.

The twentieth century saw both the multiplication of printed Qur'ans and the creation of something close to a "standard edition." In the early 1920s al-Azhar University assembled a small group of experts to produce a printed edition, subsequently revised in 1924, that has become among the most widely disseminated in the decades since its production. Often called the "Cairo edition" or "King Fu'ad edition," it remains the basis for later editions and for most subsequent English translations.

When did the Qur'an arrive in America?

On January 4, 2007, the Qur'an became the center of a controversy when the first Muslim ever elected to Congress, Representative Keith Ellison, a Democrat from Minnesota, asked to place his hand on it while taking his oath of office. Ellison used a copy of the Qur'an that had been owned by Thomas Jefferson, an English translation done in 1734 by George Sale. Conservative media outlets decried Ellison's choice, and one congressman complained that when an oath is taken to serve this country, "America is interested in only one book, the Bible." Behind all the objections lay the assertion that the Qur'an has nothing to do with America, that it's a foreign, alien entity.

But the Qur'an has a long American history. Some scholars speculate that it may have been carried by those accompanying some of the earliest explorers of what is now the continental United States. Spain had been a major Muslim region, and men of Muslim background formed part of the Spanish expeditions. Moving forward to the pre-Revolutionary period, research now indicates that the Qur'an probably arrived in colonial America on slave ships, most likely as an oral scripture held in the minds and memories of West African captives. Missionaries and traders had brought Islam to the western coast of Africa centuries before. While most Muslim slaves were unlettered, history records several who either left written records or were themselves the subject of written accounts.

One prominent example of this group is Yarrow Mamout (d. 1823). While the circumstances of his capture are unknown, Mamout was transported to the colonies in 1752. He spent more than four decades enslaved on a Maryland tobacco plantation but was eventually manumitted. Sometime after that, he moved to the Georgetown section of Washington, D.C., started a business, and built a house there. Mamout owes part of his fame to the portrait that Charles Willson Peale (who also painted Washington, Franklin, and Hamilton) did of him, a painting that now hangs in the Philadelphia Museum of Art.

Omar Ibn Sa'id (or Sayyid) (d. 1864), also transported from West Africa, worked as a slave in the Carolinas for various owners. At the request of his final master, James Owens of Fayetteville, Omar penned a brief autobiography, producing the only extant American slave memoir written in Arabic. His account begins with an extended passage from Q 67 and gives ample demonstration of his devotion and religious learning. Ibn Sa'id's manuscript, although widely disseminated during his lifetime, was eventually lost. It surfaced late in the twentieth century and was eventually purchased at auction from a private collector by the Library of Congress.

Other evidence of the Qur'an's presence in this country can be found in the writings—and the book collections—of some of our Founding Fathers. I've already mentioned the translation that Thomas Jefferson owned. This, too, is in the Library of Congress. The Boston Public Library's Rare Book Room holds a copy of a Qur'an that belonged to John Adams. It was printed in Springfield, Massachusetts, in 1806, the first translation to be published in the United States.

Throughout the nineteenth century, reference to the Qur'an and to Islamic literature can be found in the works of noted writers, such as Edgar Allan Poe (d. 1849), Washington Irving (d. 1859), and Ralph Waldo Emerson (d. 1882). They, and many other writers, artists, and intellectuals, were intrigued by "Oriental" cultures, philosophies, and religious practices.

How has the Internet affected the teaching and transmission of the Qur'an?

For good or for ill, religion has invaded the Internet. Believers in many traditions can pray and worship online, can counsel and support each other, can confront and provoke each other, and can locate resources for study and learning that were previously inaccessible. The Internet has become a vast repository of religious misinformation and a battleground of polemic and debate. It's as easy to find virulent anti-Muslim (and anti-Christian and anti-Jewish) tirades as it is to find recipes for lasagna or knitting patterns. For the dissemination of the Qur'an and for teaching and study aids, the Internet offers assets that have opened the text to huge new audiences. Sources on the Internet benefit novices and scholars alike.

Texts of the Qur'an can be searched in both Arabic and in the translations that have been made into numerous languages. For example, the Qur'anic Arabic Corpus (http://corpus.quran.com/), produced by the University of Leeds, provides sophisticated linguistic tools to facilitate the study of the Arabic text. Almost twenty years ago, the Royal Aal al-Bayt Institute for Islamic Thought in Amman, Jordan, set up a site that hosted digitized versions of major classical commentaries on the Qur'an (https://www.altafsir.com/). Several of its online commentaries are available in English translation, offering non-Arabic speakers an introduction to the vast field of qur'anic interpretation.

For those who will read the Qur'an in translation, several sites offer a search capability of versions in many languages. For example, Global Qur'an (http://globalquran.com/) collates translations in dozens of languages, everything from English, French, Spanish, and German to Swahili, Bahasa Indonesia, and Turkish. Similar functionality is available with Qur'an Explorer (http://www.quranexplorer.com/) and Tanzil (http://tanzil.net/). The latter has a particularly good recitation capacity, allowing a broad choice of reciters and setting the number of times that the reciter repeats a verse—a boon to those who are trying to memorize the Qur'an. There is even oral recitation available for the English, Persian, and Azerbaijani translations.

Such aural components on these websites—and many others—have opened qur'anic study, especially the study of recitation (known in Arabic as *tajwid*) to countless people who could never afford the time or money to attend a course of study in a mosque school or university. In addition to the study options, sites like YouTube can now give a renowned Qur'an reciter a global audience. Simply type "Quran recitation" into the site's search bar and you can sample dozens of the most famous.

Now that virtually every famous museum and major library has a website on which to display digitized treasures from their respective collections, the world of qur'anic manuscripts has opened up as never before. Here are a few sites, among many others, that are worth browsing for the their manuscript collections: the Chester Beatty Library in Dublin (http://www.cbl.ie/), the Walters Art Museum in Baltimore (https://thewalters.org/), the Museum of Islamic Art in Doha (http://www.mia.org.qa/en/), and the Museum of Turkish and Islamic Arts in Istanbul (http://www.kultur.gov. tr/EN-113954/istanbul---turkish-and-islamic-arts-museum. html). Beautiful qur'anic calligraphy is not confined to precious manuscripts; it also decorates major architectural monuments, both ancient and modern. Among the most famous of these is the Taj Mahal, the tomb complex that the Mughal emperor Shah Jahan (r. 1628–1658) built for his beloved, Mumtaz Mahal. An open-access site maintained by the Massachusetts Institute of Technology and the Agha Khan Trust for Culture (https://archnet.org/) provides photos of some of the stunning qur'anic inscriptions that decorate the mausoleum.

PART V

WHAT DOES THE QUR'AN
SAY ABOUT . . . ?

This book's final section rapidly surveys many topics, all of which are frequently raised and discussed in the popular media. Some of these subjects, such as veiling, martyrs (often in the guise of suicide bombers), female genital mutilation, and forms of severe punishment, regularly generate sensationalist coverage and heated debate. In an effort to counter distortions and misinformation, I will present basic information on these topics as clearly and succinctly as possible. While recognizing that the coverage is necessarily limited, I hope that it provides a foundation for readers to explore and investigate further. It is important to understand, however, that as Muslim thinkers of all eras deal with these matters, they do not restrict themselves to the Qur'an alone. The sayings and deeds of the Prophet Muhammad (hadith) present another essential source, as does the developed corpus of Islamic law. A final caveat: what follows should not be taken as the final word on anything. These brief surveys do not constitute a catechism on "what the Qur'an teaches" or on "what Muslims believe." They neither exhaust the infinite variety of Muslim thought and practice, both past and present, nor pretend to be prescriptive in any way. They simply offer an opening into the Qur'an as it connects with subjects of vital contemporary importance.

What does the Qur'an say about women?

People are often surprised to hear that Mary, the mother of Jesus, is the only woman actually named in the Qur'an. Other women appear in the text—Adam's wife, the woman who tempted the prophet Joseph, the woman who saved the infant Moses, the Queen of Sheba—but names were supplied for these others only in later Islamic literature. Commentaries on the Qur'an also connected certain passages to women, such as Muhammad's wives. But it is Mary, for whom the nineteenth sura of the Qur'an is named, who figures most prominently as an identified female figure.

The Qur'an has much to say about gender and gender relations in the fourth sura, entitled "The Women," and in many other places. Overall the attention is mixed. A much-quoted verse, using a series of parallels, extols women's spiritual equality with men: "Men who surrender to God, and women who surrender, and men who believe and women who believe, and men who obey and women who obey, and men who speak the truth and women who speak the truth, and men who persevere (in righteousness) and women who persevere, and men who are humble and women who are humble, and men who give alms and women who give alms . . ." (Q 33:35). Both women and men will be judged for their good and evil deeds and will merit Paradise (or not) on the basis of that judgment.

But social, legal, and—to a large extent—economic equality do not match this promise of spiritual equity. As just noted, most women in the Qur'an are known only as "wife of." While they have certain rights, those are not the same rights as men. For example, it takes two women to equal the evidentiary weight of one male witness (Q 2:282). Men may initiate divorce and may even divorce a woman unilaterally. Men may also have up to four wives simultaneously, while women must be monogamous. Men may marry non-Muslim women (Christians and Jews), but women may not marry non-Muslim men. Inheritance regulations strongly favor the male heirs, although it is often argued that men usually bear more financial responsibility than women.

Such is also the interpretation ordinarily given for a defining verse about gender relations: "Men are in charge of women, because God has made the one of them to excel the other, and because they spend of their property (for the support of women)" (Q 4:34). While the phrase "God has made the one of them to excel the other" has been used to argue the subsidiary status of women, the second half of this same verse proves even more troubling to contemporary Muslim women. It states: "So good women are the obedient, guarding in secret what God has guarded. As for those from whom you fear rebellion, admonish them and banish them to beds apart, and scourge them. Then if they obey you, do not seek a way against them. God is ever high exalted, great." What does "scourge them" mean? Is the Qur'an condoning or even promoting wife-beating? Debate about this verse has gone on for centuries but has gained intensity in the past few decades. The Arabic word here translated as "scourge" can mean anything from a light tap to a painful strike. Contemporary commentators tend to stress the former, seeking a way to reconcile this qur'anic injunction with a more egalitarian understanding of marriage relations.

Leading the way in such interpretations stands a new generation of feminist scholars and interpreters of the Qur'an. As many more women, both in the Muslim world and in Muslim diaspora communities, continue on to advanced university studies, they are becoming experts in all the subject areas required for the scholarly interpretation of the Qur'an.

What does the Qur'an say about veiling and separation?

Few aspects of Muslim culture and practice have generated more controversy than female body coverings and gender segregation. The veil—actually a headscarf—is the most visible marker of Muslim identity and a catalyst for gendered political statements and actions.

While the Qur'an does not specify precise forms of female dress, it does enjoin modesty on both men and women: "Tell the believing men to lower their gaze and be modest. That is purer for them. God is aware of what they do. / And tell the believing women to lower their gaze and be modest" (Q 24:30–31). The second verse in this passage, however, goes on to counsel women not to display themselves ("their adornment") to those other than their husbands and close relatives. The focus is on propriety between men and women as conveyed through dress and decorum and as reinforced through physical separation of the sexes.

The Qur'an uses various terms to denote such separation, but one, *hijab*, has become the most common designation for current codes of Islamic dress. Q 33:53 employs this term in referring to the etiquette required for the Prophet's household: "And when you ask of them (the wives of the Prophet) anything, ask it of them from behind a curtain (*hijab*). That is purer for your hearts and for their hearts." A few verses later, Muhammad's wives and daughters and "the women of the believers" are told "to draw their cloaks close around themselves (when they go abroad)" (Q 33:59). These specific references to the Prophet's family have caused many to question whether such commands were intended only for that time and place or for all women.

In contemporary Western usage, hijab usually means a headscarf, although in some cases the term refers to the full range of women's dress options. These include the all-encompassing body cloak (*abaya* or *burqa*) that is standard in the Gulf States; the face veil (*niqab*), with or without a transparent covering for the eyes, that is often worn by the most conservative women; and the tunic plus loose pants that is quite common in Southeast Asia.

Decisions about what forms of "Islamic dress" to adopt are ordinarily shaped, or mandated, by local social mores, and many Muslim societies have seen a full pendulum swing in the postcolonial decades of the twentieth and early twenty-first centuries. Turkish republicans banned the veil in the 1920s, and a decade later Reza Shah Pahlavi (r. 1925–1941) did so in Iran. Many Egyptian women discarded the veil midcentury in a demonstration of personal autonomy and modernization. A generation later, many were dismayed to see their daughters returning to headscarves and other forms of Islamic dress.

While some Muslim societies, such as Saudi Arabia and Iran, have made hijab a legal requirement for women, most leave the choice up to the individual, a choice that is often more easily exercised in large urban environments than in traditional rural ones. Among these, as well as among Muslim populations in Europe, North America, and elsewhere, women offer a range of reasons for choosing to wear hijab. Some seek to express their Muslim identity with this very visible marker. Others wish to make a countercultural statement, rejecting the sexualized consumerism of much Western culture. Yet others find that wearing hijab creates a "safe space" in the public sphere, deflecting unwanted attention and advances.

What does the Qur'an say about polygyny?

Muslim law permits a man to marry up to four women simultaneously, but in modern societies this practice is the exception rather than the norm. The decisive verse is Q 4:3: "And if you fear that you will not deal fairly by the orphans, marry of the women, who seem good to you, two or three or four; and if you fear that you cannot do justice (to so many) then one (only) or (the captives) that your right hands possess." Four wives as the maximum refers to four free women, while the phrase "your right hand possesses" is usually understood as slaves (i.e., women captured as war booty). A key moral injunction of this permission is the mandate for equity. All wives must be treated fairly in terms of their material maintenance, their sexual access, and provision for their children.

The verse's statement, "if you fear that you cannot do justice (to so many), then one (only)" has therefore prompted some nineteenth- and twentieth-century commentators and reformers to argue that this subsequent phrase nullifies or abrogates the original permission for four. A verse found later in the same sura bolsters the argument with its opening phrase, "You will not be able to deal equally between (your) wives, however much you wish (to do so)" (Q 4:129).

This permission for polygyny has generated continuous Western criticism and also a good deal of salacious interest, as manifest in the harem fantasies of eighteenth- and nineteenth-century European and American painters. It's worth noting the circumstances of its promulgation since Muslim tradition does provide a context. Dozens of Muslim men were killed in a battle against the Meccans at Uhud in 625, leaving scores of widows and orphans. Marriage to these women was seen as a social duty, a way of providing protection and support for them.

The abrogation arguments mentioned earlier have prompted legal changes in some Muslim countries, notably Turkey and Tunisia, where polygyny has been prohibited. Elsewhere the practice is often determined by wealth and social status. Viewed globally, it is fair to say that most Muslim men struggle to support one wife, so contracting multiple marriages may be a theoretical possibility for them but not a practical one.

Quite a few countries have instituted laws that effectively restrict polygyny. Some, for example, permit a woman to include a clause in her marriage contract that prevents her husband from taking another wife. Others require a man to secure his first wife's permission and to provide proof from legal and /

or religious authorities that the permission has been freely granted. It is worth noting, however, that such legal restrictions do not entirely prevent the practice, since it can be easy to elude official scrutiny. Western countries that have received significant immigration from the Muslim world are now grappling with the reality of polygyny within their own social systems. One pressing issue is the inability of second and third wives, who are legally married in their countries of origin, to have their marriages recognized in Europe and North America where they now reside.

What does the Qur'an say about abortion and birth control?

While the Qur'an repeatedly affirms the sanctity of human life, the words for abortion that appear in later legal literature do not occur in the text. Q 17:31, however, presents a strong condemnation of infanticide: "Do not slay your children, fearing a fall to poverty, We shall provide for them and for you. The slaying of them is great sin." A passage to be found much later in the text (Q 81:8) specifically denounces a form of infanticide apparently practiced in pre-Islamic Arabia, the live burial or exposure of infant girls. While such denunciations figure in the legal and ethical discussions of abortion, the qur'anic stress on the importance of human life and its preservation most decisively shapes this discussion. Q 4:93 proclaims God's anger against the murderer, testifying that God "has cursed him and prepared for him an awful doom."

Although recognizing that anti-abortion positions exist in both traditions, most scholars consider Judaism and Islam to be more accepting of abortion, in defined and limited circumstances, than the Christian tradition. Unlike Roman Catholic teaching, for example, Muslim legal scholars do not categorically reject abortion, although they universally regard it as blameworthy. Yet most will permit abortion in defined circumstances during specific stages of gestational development. Consequently, much of their discussion centers on the stages of conception and gestation and on how to determine when the fetus becomes viable and when the quality of personhood can be ascribed to it.

In the contemporary Muslim world the translation of religious law to current law codes varies considerably. A number of Muslim-majority countries permit abortion beyond four months of gestation only when the life of the mother is threatened. They may allow more latitude before the fourth month, but few sanction abortion "on demand" or for social and economic reasons. Only a handful of countries authorize abortion in the case of fetal impairment, but that number can be expected to grow as diagnostic technology continues to advance.

As with abortion, nothing in the Qur'an speaks directly to the practice of birth control. For relevant textual sources, medieval Muslim scholars turned to the hadith, the sayings and deeds of Muhammad and his closest companions. Those most pertinent concern the acceptability of withdrawal or coitus interruptus. An important qualification, however, and one that is also recorded in the hadith, cautions the husband to use such a form of contraception only with the wife's permission. Despite this, not all jurists give consent to the practice of birth control. Some point to Q 16:72 and similar verses that glorify a growing family as a divine blessing: "And God has given you wives of your own kind, and has given you, from your wives, sons and grandsons, and has made provision of good things for you." Nevertheless, most contemporary legal scholars sanction modern forms of contraception, deeming them to be analogous to coitus interruptus, as long as both husband and wife agree.

What does the Qur'an say about circumcision and female genital mutilation?

Male circumcision, the removal of the foreskin of the penis, has been a time-honored practice in Muslim societies. While it is not explicitly mentioned in the Qur'an, numerous hadith record and sanction the practice and, in some instances, link it to the prophet Abraham. Its apparent prevalence within pre-Islamic societies on the Arabian Peninsula may account for its presence within early Muslim communities and, consequently, the attention that it receives in hadith. In the codification of Muslim law, circumcision assumes a prominent place as a required or recommended practice. Legal manuals treat it as part of the physical purification that prepares the human body for prayer. Although widespread in the Muslim world, it is not universal, and there are communities, such as those in northwest China, where circumcision is not practiced.

Customs about the of the practice vary considerably among Muslim countries and cultures. For example, Muslims in Europe and North America generally have the operation performed by a doctor in a clinic or hospital shortly after the child's birth. In many parts of the Middle East and North Africa, however, the age of circumcision can vary from infancy to just before puberty, and surrounding rituals and celebrations can be simple or elaborate. In some traditional societies the expense of preparations and the required hospitality, with huge receptions and professional entertainment, can rival that of a wedding. Operations performed on older boys often amount to a rite of passage with accompanying expectations of unflinching endurance as a sign of toughness and manliness.

Female circumcision, now usually called female genital mutilation (FGM), also finds no mention in the Qur'an. Its sanction within Islamic law is far less secure, and the majority of Muslims do not accept the custom. In those areas of Africa and beyond where it remains entrenched, it has deep cultural roots, predating the arrival of Islam, and is also practiced by Christians and adherents of other religions. The operation itself can range from full or partial removal of the clitoris to excision and infibulation of the labia. It is extremely painful and, under the pressure exerted by human rights groups, has been outlawed in many countries. Nevertheless, it continues to exert a strong cultural hold in those places that equate family honor with a girl's virginity. Girls who have not been "circumcised" can find themselves shunned as potential marriage partners or deemed impure and unclean. Increasingly, this is becoming an American and European issue as doctors in those cities that have attracted migrants from places where the practice persists find themselves dealing with the severe medical and psychological consequences of FGM.

What does the Qur'an say about hetero- and homosexual relations?

Comparisons of Muslim and Christian attitudes toward sex frequently favor the former as conveying a more positive and joyful disposition. The qur'anic creation narrative provides no basis for a doctrine of original sin or its subsequent indictment of human nature as flawed and fallen. Celibacy is considered neither virtuous nor commendable. Sexual attraction and desire are a blessed part of God's plan but—and it's an important "but"—they can only be acted upon legitimately within a marriage: "They [women] are garments for you and you are garments for them. . . . So hold intercourse with them and seek what God has ordained for you" (Q 2:187). An obvious asymmetry operates as men may be polygamous and may initiate divorce, while women may have only a single marital relationship at a time.

Recognizing the power of human sexuality and acknowledging that illicit relationships can destroy families and friendships, the Qur'an sets some ground rules. Both men and women must dress and behave modestly, and women especially are cautioned not to "reveal their adornment" to any man except their husbands, fathers, brothers, sons, and other close male relatives (Q 24:31). The translation of these prescriptions into forms of dress and behavior has varied widely in Muslim societies across time. In the present period, the clothing choices of Muslim women can be the same as that of non-Muslims or it can be at considerable variance, depending upon region and custom.

Clothing and comportment are viewed as ways of chan-
neling human sexual impulses toward their desired end, marital love and joy, and restraining them from the forbidden acts
of adultery, incest, fornication, and prostitution. The natural
pairing of male and female is an important aspect of God's
creative activity: "O mankind! We have created you male and
female, and have made you nations and tribes that you may
know one another" (Q 49:13).

The Qur'an does not speak directly about same-sex attraction, but the story of the prophet Lot provides the basis for its
condemnation of homosexual acts. In this narrative (its biblical
counterpart is Genesis 18:16–19:29) the men of Lot's city are excoriated for lusting after other men (Q 7:80–82) and for seeking
sex with male guests to whom Lot had offered hospitality (Q
54:37). A reference in Q 4:15 to "those of your women who are
guilty of lewdness" has sometimes been interpreted to include
lesbian sexual activity, but most commentators maintain that
this verse and the one following it concern illicit heterosexual
relations.

The role of sexuality in Paradise both confirms and com-
plicates the earthly commendations and prohibitions. In the
afterlife, pious males will be wed to charming companions of
peerless beauty and perpetual virginity. Circling among them
will be "immortal youths" (Q 56:17; 76:19) bearing cups of
pure and blessed beverages.

Homosexual behavior remains illegal in a number of
Muslim-majority countries and is punished under anti-sodomy
and anti–public indecency laws. Punishment can be severe,
ranging from a death sentence to incarceration and heavy fines.
NGOs that concentrate on LGBTQ rights continue to track the
legal landscape worldwide, to record and report attacks against
gays, and to support efforts to decriminalize homosexual behavior. In a notorious case of using accusations of homosexuality for political purposes, a high-ranking Malaysian official
and leader of the opposition, Anwar Ibrahim, was twice jailed
on such charges until being pardoned and released in 2018.

What does the Qur'an say about domestic violence?

Physical and sexual violence against women remains a major human rights concern and a disturbing issue across the world. Discussions of this topic frequently repeat a statement and statistic attributed to Kofi Annan, the former secretary-general of the United Nations: "Violence against women and girls is a problem of pandemic proportions. At least one out of every three women around the world has been beaten, coerced into sex, or otherwise abused in her lifetime with the abuser usually someone known to her." Such violence is prevalent in every region and culture and no single factor suffices to explain its perpetuation.

The Qur'an figures in the discussions about domestic violence because of a short phrase that can be read as sanctioning it. The crucial verse is Q 4:34 cited here in full:

> Men are in charge of women, because God has made the one of them to excel the other, and because they spend of their property (for the support of women). So good women are the obedient, guarding in secret what God has guarded. As for those from whom you fear rebellion, admonish them and banish them to beds apart, and scourge them. Then if they obey you, do not seek a way against them. God is ever high exalted, great.

For many Muslim women (and men), both parts of this verse are contentious. The first part affirms male dominance on the grounds, according to many commentators, of both inherent superiority and financial responsibility. The second part, however, with its injunction to "scourge them," has been the subject of much debate. Classical commentators read this as the final step in a three-stage punishment process. First a husband should reprimand his wife. If this does not curb her "rebellion," he should sleep separately from her. Only if these two steps fail, should he have recourse to physical punishment.

The Arabic verb that is here translated as "scourge" has been interpreted to mean anything from a rough body blow to the slightest tap. Some other English translations of the Qur'an convey this range: spank lightly ('Abdullah Yusuf 'Ali), hit (M. A. S. Abdul Haleem, who glosses this as "a single slap"), and beat (A. J. Arberry).

This verse, however, must be understood within a much larger context. There are many hadith from the Prophet that stress the importance of caring for a wife both physically and financially and that frown upon physical chastisement. They recount Muhammad's devotion to his own wives and the counsels of patience and loving care that he addressed to his followers.

The Qur'an itself also contains many verses that praise the mutual love of husband and wife and the joys of marital harmony. It reckons the marital relation to be one of God's signs to humankind: "And of His signs is this: He created for you spouses from yourselves that you might find rest in them, and He ordained between you love and mercy" (Q 30:21).

Nevertheless, stricter interpretations of Q 4:34 have undermined efforts in some conservative Muslim countries to secure legal restraint against the physical abuse of women and minors. A recent and well-received book by Ayesha Chaudhry, *Domestic Violence and the Islamic Tradition*, offers an extended study of Q 4:34 and of its multiple interpretations. In her introduction to this work, she acknowledges feeling deeply disheartened to discover how resolutely "Islamic tradition" has undermined efforts to find a more egalitarian vision for Muslim women and men.

Even when laws against domestic violence exist, enforcement can be difficult and sporadic. If police are not trained to acknowledge and intervene, if hospitals do not document and report, if the justice system does not move swiftly, then women remain victims and the religious rhetoric against these crimes—whatever the religious tradition—can do very little.

What does the Qur'an say about divorce?

The Qur'an condones divorce and provides specific instructions about the process, but surrounds these injunctions with appeals for reconciliation and marital harmony. According to Q 30:21, God "created for you spouses from yourselves that you might find rest in them, and He ordained between you love and mercy." Husbands are urged to treat their wives with "kindness, for if you hate them it may happen that you hate a thing in which God has placed much good" (Q 4:19). Even if tension and disagreement arise, arbitration that is mediated by a representative from each spouse's family should be focused on reconciliation.

Despite this strong preference for unbroken marriages, the Qur'an recognizes the reality of divorce and regulates it. Only the husband can directly initiate a divorce, and the procedure is straightforward and unencumbered by judicial or legal requirements. All he must do is repeat the phrase "I divorce you" three times. He can revoke the declaration after its first two repetitions but the third invocation makes it final. After the third declaration there is a waiting period of three menstrual cycles before the divorce becomes irrevocable to assure that the wife is not pregnant. Should she discover a pregnancy, she must inform her husband. He, in turn, must provide for her during the pregnancy and for up to two years of lactation.

The Qur'an specifies all of these requirements, and others, in several parts of the text, predominantly in suras two and four, but also in Q 65, which is called "Divorce." For example, in order to foster a possible reconciliation, the three pronouncements of the divorce formula should be separated in time, not uttered in quick succession. After the final utterance, however, the divorce is considered irrevocable and the two spouses can only reconcile and remarry if the wife contracts and consummates an intervening marriage.

Divorcing a wife can also entail serious economic consequences since the husband loses any control over her marriage gifts, regardless of how valuable they are: "And if you wish to exchange one wife for another and you have given to one of them a sum of money (however great), take nothing from it" (Q 4:20). Those marriage gifts, however, create an opportunity for women to seek divorce. Although a wife cannot initiate divorce directly, she can bargain for it by renouncing her rights to all or some of these marriage gifts. Q 2:229 opens this option with its declaration that it is "no sin for either of them if the woman ransom herself."

As with other matters in Islamic law, the Qur'an is not the sole source. The Prophet's hadith represent another important basis for the eventual codification of all aspects of family law. Although modern reformist movements have attempted to address the gender inequities in the classical legal systems, personal status laws have remained largely in place, even in those Muslim countries that have adopted Western codes of civil and criminal law. Some exceptions exist, such as Tunisia and Morocco, where divorce must be initiated through the courts and polygyny has been restricted or banned.

What does the Qur'an say about food and fasting?

The Qur'an's many mentions of food and drink count them as part of God's benevolence toward his creatures on earth and as a reward bestowed upon those in Paradise. The references are both general and collective. Specific food items cited in the Qur'an range across the categories of fruits and vegetables, meat and fish, grains and spices. Q 2:61, for example, details the Israelites' desire for some dietary variety in the desert as they beg Moses to ask God to "bring forth for us of what the earth grows—of its herbs and its cucumbers and its corn and its lentils and its onions." Figs and grapes, pomegranates and dates all appear as instances of divine bounty. Rivers of water, wine, milk, and honey await the blessed in Paradise.

Just as food and drink are signs of God's goodness, humans should respond to this largesse with gratitude and moderation: "Eat of the provision of your Lord and render thanks to

Him" (Q 34:15); "eat and drink, but do not be prodigal. He does not love the prodigals" (Q 7:31). One should also be generous toward those in need: "Then eat of it and feed with it the poor unfortunate" (Q 2:28). Not doing so finds its place on the list of ways in which humans incur God's disfavor, as with this divine accusation: "But you (for your part) do not urge the feeding of the needy" (Q 89:18 and 107:3; cf. Q 74:44).

Despite the qur'anic exhortation to enjoy, in moderation, all that the earth produces, some foods and beverages are forbidden. This includes any intoxicating substance, whether food or drink, as well as specific categories of food. Q 5:3 offers a succinct summary: "Forbidden to you (for food) are carrion and blood and swine-flesh, and what has been dedicated to any other than God, and the strangled, and the dead through beating, and the dead through falling from a height, and what has been killed by (the goring of) horns, and devoured by wild beasts, except what you make lawful (by the death stroke), and what has been immolated to idols." In addition to prohibiting pork and the blood produced in butchering, this verse also specifies those circumstances that make carrion taboo. The following verse, Q 5:4, reiterates that "all good things are made lawful to you," and Q 5:5 makes meals shared among Muslims, Christians, and Jews possible: "The food of those who have received the scripture is lawful for you, and your food is lawful for them."

Methods of slaughter determine whether permitted meat may be considered lawful (*halal* in Arabic) or not: "And do not eat of that over which God's name has not been mentioned, for it is abomination" (Q 6:122). In Muslim-majority countries, such food selection and processing have been institutionalized. Butchers sell *halal* and restaurants serve it. The situation can be quite different in places like the United States, where Muslims face a bewildering range of daily choices. Kosher hot dogs are probably okay, but what about a burger at McDonalds or Burger King? Can you pick up a rotisserie chicken at the supermarket or sushi takeout at the local Japanese restaurant?

Muslims make different choices in such situations. Some restrict themselves to meat from halal butchers, while others take a more liberal attitude. When in doubt, many will eat either vegetarian or seafood dishes, although there are some differences between Sunnis and Shi'is about permissible forms of seafood.

The Qur'an encourages, and even mandates, abstaining from food under certain conditions. The most noted of these is the fast of Ramadan, a month-long ritual during which observant Muslims refrain from food, drink, and sexual activity from dawn until dusk. Fasting is also a form of repentance or compensation for some moral offenses or for failure to fulfill ritual requirements. For example, Q 4:92 sets the recompense for the unintentional murder of a believer as the manumission of a slave. Should that prove impossible, the killer "must fast two consecutive months." A famous verse (Q 33:35) that aligns the pious behaviors of men and women refers in a more general way to the ascetical practice of fasting: "men who are humble and women who are humble, and men who give alms and women who give alms, and men who fast and women who fast."

What does the Qur'an say about drinking and drugs?

Most people know that observant Muslims don't drink alcohol, so they may be surprised to learn that the Qur'an says quite a bit about wine and other intoxicants. All the qur'anic references taken together characterize wine as an earthly problem but a heavenly blessing. The qur'anic term for wine refers to a drink made from fermented grapes but, by extension, also includes other alcoholic beverages. The first hearers of the Qur'an, for example, were probably more familiar with fermented beverages made from dates, honey, or grains. They were certainly well aware of the delights of such drinks and could readily understand the attraction posed by the wines of Paradise. According to Q 47:15, the heavenly garden nourishes the blessed with manifold bounties, including "rivers of wine delicious to the drinkers." Later in the text, a very special beverage is described: "They are given to drink of a pure wine, sealed / Whose seal is musk—For this let (all) those strive who strive for bliss— / And mixed with water of Tasnīm / A spring from which those brought near (to God) drink" (Q 83:25–28). Not only is the wine of Paradise far more delicious than its earthly counterpart, it boasts another benefit: you can drink as much as you like and never get drunk. Picture the scene in Q 56 of the blessed in Paradise reclining, their goblets constantly topped up with a drink "from which they get no aching of the head nor any madness" (Q 56:19).

Earthly wine, however, is another matter. It is precisely alcohol's effects on body and mind that prompt its qur'anic prohibition. That prohibition, however, proceeds in stages and offers a textbook example of two interpretive features of the Qur'an, "occasions of revelation" and "abrogation." Classical Muslim scholars sought to identify the historical situations that coincided with Muhammad's proclamation of particular verses. By clarifying the chronology of verses, they were then able to determine how some verses of the Qur'an could nullify a verse, or verses, that had been previously revealed. Such is the case with a series of passages that mention intoxicants. Initially, ambivalence marks the combined mention of wine and gambling—"In both is great sin, and (some) utility for men; but the sin of them is greater than their usefulness" (Q 2:219)—but subsequent mentions express successive constrictions. Q 4:43 warns believers not to join the ritual prayer when inebriated, while Q 5:90–91 provide the conclusive condemnation. These verses denounce strong drink and games of chance as "Satan's handiwork" because they "turn you from remembrance of God and from (His) worship."

Although drugs, in the contemporary sense of illicit narcotics, find no mention in the Qur'an, Muslim legal scholars have consistently classed them with the intoxicants that the Qur'an forbids. Contemporary religious leaders in the Muslim world are unanimous in their denunciation of such substances. Not unexpectedly, such scholars and leaders have also proscribed any activities that promote the production, sale, and consumption of alcohol and other intoxicants under penalty of punishment. These prohibitions are enshrined in the public law of many Muslim countries.

Like other communities, Muslim communities in the United States and elsewhere struggle with the devastating effects of drug addictions, especially those created by the epidemic of prescription opioids. Religious leaders, medical professionals, and social workers have begun to convene and to work together to educate their clients, patients, and congregations and to advocate for more effective treatment and rehabilitation.

What does the Qur'an say about jihad?

Few Arabic words have become more familiar to English-speakers than the term "jihad." In popular parlance it carries only one meaning: religiously motivated war. While that meaning is not false, it is only part of the story. The word "jihad" and other related formulations may be found in forty-one verses of the Qur'an, but in only ten of those occurrences does it signify warfare. Instances of a phrase that can be translated as "striving (jihad) in the way *of* God" or "struggle (jihad) for the sake of God" signal the broader range of meanings. The core meaning of "struggle" or "striving" can apply to many kinds of efforts, both individual and collective, that the believers make to please God. These can be acts of charity, pious and prayerful practices, seeking religious knowledge, combating one's sinful impulses, and undertaking forms of spiritual purification, such as fasting and pilgrimage. This range of meanings became particularly important in the Sufi movements that developed during the classical and medieval periods. Q 22:78, which calls the believer to strive for God with the striving (jihad) that is his due, captures this more inclusive sense of the term. A famous hadith of the Prophet refers to the spiritual struggle as the "greater jihad" and to physical combat and confrontation as the "lesser jihad."

Nevertheless, the term "jihad" also means war, and in the centuries following the appearance of the Qur'an the concept of jihad has emerged as a more fully developed doctrine of warfare. This doctrine divides the world into two parts, the region or "house" of Islam and the "house of war." As classically defined, the "house of Islam" comprised all legitimately constituted Muslim governments, while the "house of war" was everyone and everyplace else. By definition, the two divisions existed in a permanent state of hostility, although truces between entities within each could be declared under restricted circumstances. Such truces eventually became the norm between Islamic and non-Islamic states.

Jihad was further defined and specified in legal texts. Provisions in the text stipulated who could or must participate in these battles. They established the grounds upon which war could be declared, such as defense of the "house of Islam" and enlargement of its borders. The law books also delineated the months during which wars may be waged, the conditions that must be offered to opponents (conversion or taxation) before fighting began, and the regulations relevant to prisoners of war and captured booty. Many modern theologians and commentators have argued that while the Qur'an does provide sanction for warfare, the intent is not to authorize unbridled aggression but to justify defensive warfare.

Throughout its history, jihad emerged as a major tool of intra-Muslim conflict. Opposition movements could legitimate their claims by declaring the established leaders to be apostates or unbelievers. This validated their religious duty to topple them from power. Gamal Abdel Nasser, the second president of Egypt, faced such charges, and radical groups attacked him for failing to establish an Islamic government. In retaliation, Nasser moved aggressively against the most influential of these groups, the Muslim Brotherhood, throwing much of their senior leadership into jail. Nasser's successor as president, Anwar Sadat, fell victim to this same intra-Muslim argument about political legitimacy and was assassinated in 1981.

What does the Qur'an say about war and terrorism?

Within the realm of classical Islamic law, the category of war draws upon a very wide range of qur'anic citations beyond those verses that deal with jihad. The relation of fighting in the promotion of God's will and the defense of his religion is a major theme in the Qur'an. Some mention of ancient wars provides the background for this. For example, the story of Saul and Goliath is used as an exemplary instance of how God supports those who do battle against overwhelming odds. The small band that stayed faithful to Saul as he approached Goliath professed their faith in God's power: "How many a little company has overcome a mighty host by God's leave!" (Q 2:249). When David slew Goliath, that faith was confirmed, and the narrative concludes with a justification of divinely sanctioned warfare: "And if God had not repelled some men by others the earth would have been corrupted" (Q 2:251). Brief references to the destruction of the first and second temples of Jerusalem (Q 17:4–7) and to the defeat of the Byzantines (Q 30:2–5) draw further lessons from past history.

Qur'anic verses require war and fighting, in defined circumstances, but also present such situations as God's test for the believers. Defending oneself, one's family, and one's community justifies fighting, but the retaliation must be commensurate with the wrong done. Q 2:190 cautions the believers to "fight in the way of God against those who fight against you, but do not begin hostilities. God does not love aggressors." But God also chastises those who shrink from the call to righteous warfare and promises heavenly rewards for those who embrace it. According to Q 4:174, "Whoever fights in the way of God, be he slain or be he victorious, on him We shall bestow a vast reward."

Two verses in the ninth sura became so central to the qur'anic and post-qur'anic theories of war that they carry their own titles, the "Sword Verse" (Q 9:5) and the "Jizya Verse" (Q 9:29). The Sword Verse states: "Then, when the sacred months have passed, slay the idolaters wherever you find them, and take them (captive), and besiege them, and prepare for them each ambush. But if they repent and establish worship and pay the poor-due, then leave their way free. God is forgiving, merciful." Classical commentators on the Qur'an insisted that it nullified or "abrogated" many of the more conciliatory verses in the Qur'an. Even here, however, the aggression is directed against those who have broken treaties and pledges of peace. The Jizya (poll tax) Verse focuses on "those who have been given the scripture," usually understood to be Jews and Christians. These groups may remain within Muslim territory if they agree to pay a head tax as a sign of their subordinate status.

Taking hostages, in the sense of holding people for ransom or to assure the fulfillment of a pledge, finds no explicit justification in the Qur'an. Nor is it treated in the classical manuals of Islamic law. Nevertheless, hostage-taking has been justified in the modern period when it forms part of a larger effort to defeat opponents. In some instances, however, the effort has been defended on political rather than religious grounds.

Terrorism is commonly defined as the use of force and violence by non-state actors, often against non-military targets and often with intent to foster fear and intimidation. There is no word for this in the Qur'an, yet, in the minds of many people today, Islam is inextricably linked with terrorism. Media images and commentaries continuously reinforce this equation, despite many instances of such violence that have nothing to do with Islam. While there is no denying that Muslims, and those of other faiths—and of no faith—have committed terrorist atrocities, their motivations are not reliably religious. Repeated condemnations of terrorist actions by major Muslim leaders are either ignored by the press or relegated to the back pages.

What does the Qur'an say about slavery?

As in the Bible, there are passages in the Qur'an that accept slavery as part of the divinely ordained social order. Both scriptures, of course, reflect their social and historical context. Q 16:71 confirms this disparity: "And God has favored some of you above others in provision. Now those who are more favored will by no means hand over their provision to those (slaves) whom their right hands possess, so that they may be equal with them in respect of it." This passage uses a frequently found qur'anic phrase for slaves (i.e., "those whom their/your right hand possesses").

As with other cultures of the Near East, slaves in sixth- and seventh-century Arabia were counted as members of the household but with a lower status than family and kin. The systems of plantation slavery that developed in the early modern period, principally in North and South America, find no textual justification in the Qur'an. Slaves occur in the list of those to whom kindness should be offered: "(Show) kindness to parents, and to near kindred, and orphans, and the needy, and to the neighbor who is related (to you) and the neighbor who is not related, and the fellow-traveler and the wayfarer and (the slaves) whom your right hands possess" (Q 4:36). Freeing slaves counts as a praiseworthy act in the Qur'an, urged upon the believers as both a kindness and a way of atoning for sins. Later Islamic law developed procedures of manumission through direct declaration or as part of a last will and testament.

The Qur'an countenances concubinage, the use of female slaves as sexual partners, and such women do not count among the four legal wives that Q 4:3 sanctions. Slave women can also become marriage partners if they are Muslim. Married slave women, however, are not subject to the same punishments for adultery for which freewomen are liable: "if when they are honorably married they commit lewdness they shall incur the half of the punishment (prescribed) for free women" (Q 4:25).

While qur'anic statements on slavery reflect its historical and geographical context, the spread of Islam in subsequent centuries entailed cultural encounters that shifted the institution of slavery. The limited domestic and agricultural slavery of the qur'anic milieu was far different from the dynastic developments of later centuries. Slave soldiers—Mamluks—were recruited to the retinues of rulers. Their expanding influence and increasing status created a political elite. At its apogee in the Mamluk sultanate (1254–1517), slave soldiers became the rulers. The later Ottoman Janissary corps, which relied on the forced conversion of Christian male slaves from the Caucasus region, formed another ruling elite built upon rigorous education and strict discipline.

West African practices of slave capture, chiefly as a consequence of intra-Islamic wars, populated the transatlantic slave ships and brought large numbers of Muslims to North America in the seventeenth and eighteenth centuries.

What does the Qur'an say about martyrs?

As in Christianity and Judaism, a martyr is one who "witnesses" to his or her faith to the point of death. The common Arabic word for martyr, *shahid,* carries this basic sense of seeing and beholding, as well as the more specialized sense of dying for one's beliefs. Early commentators on the qur'anic passages that speak about such "witnesses" interpret them to be those who died in battle, who were "killed in God's way." In Q 57:19 they are listed along with the "pious," and in Q 4:69 they are ranked with the just, the righteous, the prophets, and those whom God favors. The initial context of this concept is the battlefield. Defensive wars against those who opposed the nascent Muslim community were a feature of the Prophet Muhammad's life and the years that followed his death.

Martyrs become a religious elite. The Qur'an promises immediate entrance to Paradise: "And those who are slain in the way of God, He does not render their actions vain / He will guide them and improve their state / And bring them in to the Garden which He has made known to them" (Q 47:4–7). The hadith expand upon this, detailing the physical delights awaiting martyrs in Paradise, the crown that will be awarded, the beautiful women whom male martyrs will enjoy, and the sumptuous feasts and fruits which will be constantly on offer. In the last several decades, the rewards promised to martyrs have been used to recruit commandos and to sustain military motivation in both national conflicts (the Iran-Iraq War) and in terrorist operations (the attacks of September 11, 2001, and the more recent attacks by ISIS).

Shi'i Islam looks back to the death of the third Imam, Husayn ibn 'Ali (d. 680), as a defining moment. Husayn, a grandson of the Prophet Muhammad, and a group of supporters and family were killed on the tenth day of the Islamic month of Muharram in 680 CE on a battleground in Iraq. The site of this martyrdom, Karbala, has become a pilgrimage destination for Shi'is who seek divine blessings at the shrine tomb of Imam Husayn. Shi'is worldwide commemorate the anniversary of Husayn's "passion" and martyrdom with public processions and performances.

Contemporary political ideologies have seized upon the concept of martyrdom to recruit fighters for struggles of nationalist resistance and for uprisings that assert the promotion of Islamic values and Shari'a-based governments against the domination of Western powers. Such recruitment is not restricted to adult males, but targets women and children as well. Some recruits become suicide bombers, attackers who strap explosives on their bodies or drive vehicles packed with ammunition and die in the effort to kill others. While most Muslims believe that suicide is an offense against God, since he alone decides a person's life span, and can cite qur'anic verses (Q 4:29–30 and 2:195) to support this condemnation, there is considerable debate about whether self-immolation is a justified tactic of war. Many consider suicide bombers to be modern martyrs, entitled to all of the earthly and heavenly honor that earlier martyrs have been accorded. Two famous Egyptian intellectuals of the twentieth-century, Hasan al-Banna (d. 1949), founder of the Muslim Brotherhood, and Sayyid Qutb (d. 1966), preached and promoted the religious blessings of martyrdom as a form of justified defiance against corrupt governments. Since al-Banna was killed by the secret police and Qutb was hanged, both are venerated as martyrs by their followers.

What does the Qur'an say about peace?

The most common formal greeting between Muslims is "Peace be upon you," to which the appropriate response is "And peace to you also." When the name of the Prophet Muhammad is uttered, it is followed by the phrase "peace and blessings be upon him." The Arabic word for "peace" (*salam*) is semantically related to both "Islam" and "Muslim" and to the notion that faithful submission to God's will creates peace in the heart of the believer and in the relations among families, friends, and societies.

Q 97, which speaks of the Qur'an's revelation to the Prophet "on the night of power," concludes with the luminous vision of "peace until the rising of the dawn." Peace suffuses the qur'anic depiction of Paradise, the "abode of peace" to which God summons those who are faithful to his guidance (Q 10:25). According to Q 56:25–26, "There they hear no vain speaking nor recrimination / (Nothing) but the saying: 'Peace,' (and again) peace." Those who enter the Garden, "underneath which rivers flow" (Q 14:23) are greeted with expressions of peace: "Enter it in peace. This is the day of immortality" (Q 50:34). One striking passage promises that God himself speaks this blessing: "Those who merit paradise this day are happily employed / They and their wives, in pleasant shade, on thrones reclining / Theirs the fruit (of their good deeds) and theirs (all) that they ask / The word from a merciful Lord (for them) is: 'Peace!'" (Q 36:54–57).

The serenity that marks Paradise must be mirrored in earthly human behavior. Q 25:63 counsels the believers to turn away taunts with peaceful rejoinders: "The (faithful) servants of the Beneficent are they who walk upon the earth modestly, and when the foolish ones address them answer: 'Peace.'" Believers are urged to repel evil deeds with good (Q41:34) and when angered, to forgive (Q 42:37) and patiently endure. Such counsels, however, do not equate to pacifism. Aggression against the Muslim community or efforts to reduce its spread must be countered with justified force. Nevertheless, the higher spiritual aspiration should be for worldwide social cooperation grounded in the absence of corruption and conflict.

Like the promised peace of Paradise, humans can experience true inner peace in this life, but only with complete submission to God's will. The word *islam* connotes this active surrender, and a *muslim* is one who surrenders. God bestows tranquility upon the human heart: "He it is who sent down peace of reassurance into the hearts of the believers that they might add faith to their faith" (Q48: 4).

What does the Qur'an say about government and politics?

The Qur'an says relatively little about rules of government and political conduct but is more explicit about legal matters, serving as a primary source for the classical formulations of Islamic law. It also sets a framework for the exercise of authority. A legitimate authority should govern with justice and should make its primary duty the promotion of the good and the eradication of evil.

According to the Qur'an, all human authority is derived from divine authority. Only God possesses full and absolute authority. He is "the Lord of the worlds" (Q 1:2) and to him "belongs the sovereignty of the heavens and the earth" (Q 5:40).

While God delegates authority to his prophets and messengers, delegation beyond that group has always been a contested issue. A key verse in this ongoing debate is Q 4:59, which commands the believers to obey God, the messenger (Muhammad), and "those of you who are in authority." Commentators have explained that final phrase in various ways. For some it refers to the Prophet's close companions, some of whom became future caliphs. Others apply the reference to religious scholars, while yet others expand the interpretation to include those who rule Muslim countries and communities. Within the Shi'i commentary tradition, this phrase connotes the line of infallible imams, the spiritual leaders of the community who stand in the Prophet's bloodline.

A union of political and religious leadership remains the ideal for the Muslim community. Such a union is modeled on the life of Muhammad, who served both functions for the nascent Muslim community in Medina. While Islamic political philosophy continues to espouse this united form of leadership, it clearly recognizes the separation of roles that emerged early in the centuries following the Prophet's death.

That separation has become more pronounced in the modern period, particularly in Muslim countries that experienced a prolonged period of colonial rule. During their colonial periods, many of these countries adopted primary codes of law based on European models and confined the implementation of religious law to matters of personal status (i.e., marriage and divorce, inheritance, and other family matters).

This bifurcation troubles those religious reformers who view it as an abrogation of the primacy of God's overriding authority. For them, the divinely ordained Shari'a should serve as the basis of human society: "And now We have set you (Muhammad) on a clear road (Shari'a) of our commandment; so follow it, and do not follow the whims of those who know not" (Q 45:18) Full implementation of the Shari'a would, according to Muslim political theorists like Sayyid Qutb (d. 1966) and Ayatollah Khomeini (d. 1989), assure a just and equitable social order. While a role is allotted to human judgment, especially that formed by consultation (*shura'* in Arabic) with the religious authorities, ultimately such judgment remains subordinate to divine authority. Leaders who refuse to acknowledge this and grant power to themselves are open to charges of apostasy and subject to the punishment that such a charge incurs.

What does the Qur'an say about democracy?

The ill-fated Arab Spring of 2011 resurrected the debate about Islam and democracy, re-engaging positions that have deep roots. Not surprisingly, the Qur'an says nothing about democracy as "government by the people and for the people." Rather, it continually asserts that all true authority derives from God. Nevertheless, political thinkers, particularly in the modern period, have identified points of connection between core aspects of democratic practice and foundational principles of Islamic legal theory.

The forty-second sura of the Qur'an is named after the verse that speaks approvingly of those "whose affairs are a matter of counsel" (Q 42:38), with "counsel" being explained as formalized consultation and deliberation. Clearly, various electoral processes can be understood as compatible with this principle. The more contested issues are those areas where diverse interpretations can be drawn from key qur'anic verses: the scope of divine law (Shari'a), the legal inequality of men and women, the status of non-Muslim minorities, and specified corporal punishments.

Interpretive opinions on these matters cover a very broad spectrum indeed. Thinkers like the Pakistani jurist and philosopher Abu A'la al-Mawdudi (d. 1979) refuse to grant any actual authority to elected officials. For them, political governance in accord with Islamic law could not be determined by rulers or elected representatives but only by religious scholars, those with the requisite training to interpret Islamic law. Other intellectuals advocate a limited democracy as an antidote to despotism. The Iranian philosopher Abdolkarim Soroush would go much further in supporting popular sovereignty and relegating religious authority to a more restricted role.

Some reformist efforts seek to align their societies with international human rights covenants. Others emphasize egalitarian and inclusive aspects of the Qur'an. Many choose to stress those elements of religion that maintain moral order in society and restrict human conduct that might disrupt this order. Larger historical and political forces shape and structure this debate in the contemporary world. These include the creation of nation-states in the aftermath of the colonial era and the potent mix of modernization, Westernization, and globalization that has transformed every Muslim-majority country. Regional wars and revolutions—the ongoing Israel-Palestine conflict, the 1979 Iranian revolution, the US-led invasions of Iraq and Afghanistan—play major roles both in fueling Muslim opposition to liberal democracy and in reinforcing the arguments of those who insist that democracy is the only viable future for flourishing Muslim societies.

When mapping current Muslim-majority countries on an axis of most democratic to least, political scientists estimate that about one-third of Muslims live in countries that can be classed as democratic, such as Indonesia, Turkey, Mali, Senegal, and Albania. A large number—about 150 million—constitute substantial minority populations in democratic societies like India, Europe, and North America. The regions that most people associate with Islam (i.e., the Middle East and North Africa [MENA]) do not fare well on the democracy index. While some, like Egypt, Jordan, Iran, and Morocco, go through (sometimes constrained) election processes, most MENA nations have authoritarian regimes or monarchies with serious limitations on the individual liberties and civil rights that characterize well-functioning democracies.

What does the Qur'an say about international relations?

While the Qur'an provides little detail about the larger international milieu within which it originated, it does address such matters as war and peace, sovereignty, political control, and diplomacy. Certain events in the life of the nascent Muslim community to which qur'anic verses are tied set the precedents and protocols for the conduct of warfare, the negotiation of truces, the treatment of prisoners, and other matters relevant to international relations. For example, the first verse of Q 48, titled "The Victory," is often interpreted to refer to a favorable truce forged between Muhammad and his community in Medina and the Quraysh tribe in Mecca: "We have given you (O Muḥammad) a signal victory." By the terms of this truce, the Prophet and his followers were to be provided access to Mecca at a certain time in order to perform the hajj.

Qur'anic principles that frame the Muslim approach to international relations include the concept of a worldwide Muslim community, the mandate for Islam's global expansion, and the lack of separation between religion and state. Following upon the theological dictate that God is one, so too should the Muslim community, the *umma* in Arabic, be one united people. Judaism speaks of such unity as the "people of Israel," and Christianity calls it the "universal church." The Muslim notion of umma erases distinctions of nationality and of race, class, and caste. Q 3:110 captures this with the declaration: "You are the best community that has been raised up for mankind. You enjoin right conduct and forbid indecency; and you believe in God." Other qur'anic verses refer to a "middle" or balanced community, a model of how human society should relate to God. Of course, Muslims recognize the enormous plurality and heterogeneity of the contemporary world of Islam, the diversity of national identities, and the vastly different forms of government and social organization. Nevertheless, as an ideal, the concept of a single, united Muslim community endures.

Translating Muslim unity into modern institutional structures fostered the formation of pan-Islamic ideologies and organizations. Intellectual and political trends that emerged in
the later part of the nineteenth century, and continued well
into the twentieth, stressed the totality of the Muslim world,
seeking to distinguish it from the particularity of nation-
states and from the divisive effects of Western colonialism.
Contemporary organizations like the Muslim World League
and the Organization of Islamic Cooperation continue to emphasize the unity of the Muslim community and function as a
form of intra-Islamic international relations.

Like Christianity, Islam is a missionary religion, seeking to
convert others to the final revelation that God has granted to humankind and to create a global social and political order that acknowledges the sovereignty of God. Yet the diversity of peoples
and groups also receives positive mention in the Qur'an: "O mankind! We have created you male and female, and have made you
nations and tribes that you may know one another" (Q 49:13).

The ideal world-encompassing community would be one
of universal peace and justice, but achieving that goal can involve both defensive and aggressive battle. The qur'anic passages about warfare are complex and diverse, ranging from
those that command territorial expansion to those that urge
peaceful relations, and all of them must be read against the
very different historical situation of seventh-century Arabia.
A further distinction is made between those, like Jews and
Christians, who acknowledge the one God and those who do
not. Within the contemporary world, Muslim political theorists recognize the necessity of peaceful coexistence and engage
in the debate around international codes and covenants such
as the Universal Declaration of Human Rights.

What does the Qur'an say about environmentalism?

The Muslim world is alive with efforts to harness scriptural
resources to combat the major problems of environmental

destruction and degradation. The religion and ecology movement that began in the 1980s and 1990s drew contributions from Muslim scholars and religious leaders. Even before that, prominent intellectuals like the University of Chicago professor Fazlur Rahman (d. 1988) and the Shi'i scholar Seyyed Hossein Nasr wrote about humans' relation to the natural world. Their work and that of others draws upon fundamental qur'anic principles, such as the responsibility of humans to be stewards of nature, the unity and equality of all creation as the act of one Creator, the core values of moderation and justice, and the essential purpose of nature to praise God and to offer countless signs (*ayat* in Arabic) of his grace and mercy. Q 6:166, for example, announces human stewardship with "He it is who has placed you as viceroys of the earth," a declaration confirmed in Q 27:62, Q 35:39, and elsewhere. Q 32:7 stresses the goodness of God's creation ("Who made all things good which He created") and Q 7:56 encourages the preservation of nature's bounty: "Do not work confusion in the earth after the fair ordering (of it), and call on Him in fear and hope. The mercy of God is near to the good."

Yet another key qur'anic passage, Q 33:72, and one closely linked to the concept of stewardship, affirms human responsibility for the natural world but with a harsh criticism: "We offered the trust to the heavens and the earth and the hills, but they shrank from bearing it and were afraid of it. And man assumed it. He has proved a tyrant and a fool." Importantly, this verse defines the primary principle of humanity's relationship to nature to be one of care and protection, not dominion.

Building upon these qur'anic mandates, Muslim environmental organizations—local, national, and international— have sprung up around the world. They take many forms, but all endeavor to raise public awareness and to promote changes that can ameliorate environmental damage. Some also lobby for policies that support ecological justice, particularly for those countries—many of them Muslim-majority—that will suffer disproportionately from rising sea levels and other disastrous effects of climate change. In 1994 a British Muslim activist, Fazlun Khalid, founded the Islamic Foundation for Ecology and Environmental Science (IFEES). Its website points directly to Q 6:166 (see earlier discussion) as the qur'anic warrant for its work. IFEES publishes teaching and training materials, such as its "Green Guide," a booklet that includes a checklist to assess "How Green Is My Family?" An important part of its work has been facilitating the production and dissemination of the *Islamic Declaration on Global Climate Change*, a document first promulgated on August 18, 2015, at a conference in Istanbul attended by NGOs, scholars, UN representatives, and leaders of interfaith organizations.

In the United States, the Islamic Society of North American (ISNA), this country's largest Muslim organization, is promoting its ISNA Green Initiative. During Ramadan, for example, it calls for mosques and Islamic centers to avoid food and water waste, use biodegradable paper products, recycle material, replace old light bulbs with energy-efficient ones, and preach sermons on the Islamic duty to conserve and protect the environment.

What does the Qur'an say about financial transactions?

Many passages in the Qur'an address economic and financial matters, covering everything from trade and commerce to personal inheritance to public taxation to interest and financial risk. So pervasive is the marketplace terminology of the Qur'an that metaphors based on commercial transactions are used to express key ethical and theological teachings. The universal familiarity of business life made it an apt way to convey ideas about profit and loss in human life, like God's weighing human deeds on a scale to see if the good outweigh the bad.

In the Qur'an, the same principles that govern social interactions—justice, fairness, moderation, and care for the needy—should govern matters of commerce and finance. Unbridled capitalism is not the qur'anic message, but neither is the renunciation of all commercial gain. The emphasis on moderation, on finding a balance between excessive consumption and dire poverty, underlies the qur'anic prohibition of interest-bearing loans or of loans that charge excessive interest. The equivocation in the last sentence arises because the Arabic word *riba* can mean both interest and usury (i.e., excessive interest). Consequently, debate developed among Muslim scholars about the extent of the qur'anic prohibition, and it remains a matter of disagreement. The Qur'an argues against (excessive) interest on the grounds that it promotes the unfair acquisition of wealth at the expense of economic justice. It takes advantage of the disadvantaged (i.e., the debtor). To emphasize this point, Q 30:39 contrasts usury with charity: "What you give in usury in order that it may increase on (other) people's property has no increase with God; but what you give in charity, seeking God's countenance, has increase manifold."

Given the strong and repeated prohibition against interest, how can Muslims and Muslim countries participate in the international economic order? After all, the contemporary global economy runs on credit and interest-bearing loans. The response to that question has been both theoretical and practical. In the nineteenth century, with the impact of Western colonialism, Muslim intellectuals began to explore the possible intersections between Islamic thought and modern economics. In the mid-twentieth century, a school of Islamic economics emerged that argued for the value of interest prohibition and of religiously required almsgiving as powerful factors in the promotion of social justice and economic equity.

More practically, the past half century has witnessed the emergence of Islamic banks across the Muslim world, a small but rapidly growing sector of the worldwide financial system. Some global financial institutions, such as Citibank and HSBC, offer forms of Islamic banking. In order to operate within the constraints of the qur'anic prohibition of interest, these banks use mechanisms of profit sharing to rebalance the risk of loan transactions. Interest-free financing, for example, could entail the bank's purchasing a house and reselling it to the client at a price that replicates the profit received through conventional mortgages. Refocusing the financial relationship to one of shared risk or partnership, rather than the asymmetry of creditor-debtor, has reconfigured many other commercial vehicles within the world of Islamic finance.

What does the Qur'an say about justice?

The concept of justice is so central to qur'anic teaching that it ties together God's actions of creation and judgment. God made the universe with truth and justice and decreed that every human would be judged on the basis of good or evil deeds: "And God has created the heavens and the earth with truth, and that every soul may be repaid what it has earned. And they will not be wronged" (Q 45:22). The urgent preaching of Muhammad's first years as a prophet were filled with exhortations to just action. He targeted the social and economic inequities of Meccan society, arguing for the rights of the poor, the widowed, and the orphaned, and severely criticizing those who accumulated wealth at the expense of the needy. A verse in the fourth sura captures the divine command: "O you who believe! Be staunch in justice, witnesses for God, even though it be against yourselves or (your) parents or (your) kindred, whether (the case be of) a rich man or a poor man, for God is nearer to both (than you are). So do not follow passion for fear that you lapse (from truth) and if you lapse or fall away, then God is ever informed of what you do" (Q 4:125).

The Qur'an talks about justice—and injustice—from three perspectives: how it should operate in actions between humans, how it characterizes God's dealings with humans, and how God's justice is a quality of God's being. Recognizing that humans do not always treat each other fairly, the Qur'an addresses everything from commercial transactions, to judicial procedures, to the intimate relations among family members. Frequent admonitions caution the wealthy and powerful about the punishments awaiting those who use their status to take advantage of the least privileged members of society.

God demands just action from his human creation and, through his revelation, helps them to understand how this should operate in the specifics of human life. A key passage is Q 16:90: "God enjoins justice and kindness, and giving to kinsfolk, and forbids lewdness and abomination and wickedness. He exhorts you in order that you may take heed." Through the many qur'anic counsels to treat people fairly, God lays the foundation for his role as final judge. On the Last Day, he will hold each person to account for deeds, just and unjust, good and bad, performed over an entire lifetime.

That judgment will be characterized by God's own inherent justice. In a notable metaphor, Q 4:40 uses the weight of a tiny ant to accentuate divine fairness: "God does no wrong even of the weight of an ant; and if there is a good deed, He will double it and will give (the doer) from His presence an immense reward." In later Islamic theology, the idea of God's absolute justice became a debatable proposition. It argued questions like: Is an action just because God decrees it, or does God decree it because it is just?

What does the Qur'an say about punishment?

Punishment looms large in the Qur'an. Humans can experience punishment in this life and perhaps in the next. God acts in history, and these actions can have dire consequences for humans. God also mandates particular punishments for certain grave offenses.

Woven throughout the Qur'an are a series of stories that dramatically underscore the devastating effects of divine wrath. As a collection, these have come to be called "the punishment stories," and they present a pattern that repeats from one prophetic era to the next. The seventh sura of the Qur'an, for example, includes a succession of such stories, dealing with figures from ancient Arabian lore (Hud, Salih, Shu'ayb) and those found in the Bible (Noah, Lot, and Moses). These narratives typically depict a prophet's fruitless efforts to persuade his people to reform their ways and turn in obedience to the one God. Their rejection of the prophet's message and persistence in unbelief inevitably prompt divine retribution.

The qur'anic accounts of Moses and Pharaoh provide an especially vivid example of this genre. As Pharaoh rebuffs Moses' repeated attempts to free his people from Egyptian enslavement and oppression, God intervenes with plagues and other punishments that finally emancipate the Children of Israel and vindicate the message of Moses. A twentieth-century telling of this qur'anic episode figures significantly in the political propaganda of Islamist opposition groups. Denouncing a ruling regime as tyrannical unbelievers on the model of Pharaoh and his court allows such movements to don the mantle of Moses as a righteous freedom fighter.

In the context of the Qur'an, these punishment stories function as both admonition and encouragement: they warn those who reject Muhammad's message of the consequences of their disbelief, while at the same time, they hearten his followers to withstand persecution and trust in God's eventual vindication.

As God's message to humankind, the Qur'an deals directly with the rules that direct human behavior. It sets boundaries and demarcations for what counts as praiseworthy and what counts as blameworthy. While a final reckoning for the deeds of a person's life is left to the Day of Judgment, the Qur'an does specify the punishments for certain offenses. In modern times, these have become the focus of considerable controversy and anti-Muslim sentiment. In Q 24:2: "The adulteress and the adulterer, scourge each one of them (with) a hundred stripes. And do not let pity for the two withhold you from obedience to God, if you believe in God and the last day. And let a party of believers witness their punishment." Stoning, while not explicitly mentioned in the Qur'an, has also been inflicted as a punishment for adultery. Justification for this involves a complicated exegetical maneuver in which the actual textual reference has been removed or "abrogated" but its legal force remains.

Flogging for alcohol consumption and for false accusations of adultery fall into the category of mandated sanctions, as does the retribution for theft: "As for the thief, both male and female, cut off their hands. It is the reward of their own deeds, an exemplary punishment from God. God is mighty, wise" (Q 5:38). While this sounds barbaric, hand amputation, as well as the punishments for adultery, are enacted infrequently, just as the biblical punishments in the Book of Leviticus no longer govern for Jews and Christians. Most Muslim countries now have legislative systems modeled on European systems of law and penal codes that accord with these. Nevertheless, the Qur'an-specified punishments (known as *hudud* in Arabic) have not disappeared completely. News reports from, for example, Afghanistan (especially under the Taliban), from Saudi Arabia, and from Pakistan attest to their continued implementation. Since the offenses that occasion these punishments are considered to be crimes against the social order, they are usually justified as attempts to restore that order. As with the death penalty in the United States, proponents of these severe punishments argue that they act as a deterrent and that they forestall a society's descent into immorality and anarchy.

The final area in which the Qur'an details forms of punishment is that of the afterlife. As with the Christian doctrines of Heaven and Hell, the torments of the damned in the fires of Hell are depicted in graphic detail.

What does the Qur'an say about Jews?

The Qur'an expresses ambivalent views about the Jews and Judaism, with some passages acknowledging them as believers, while others condemn their perfidy and infidelity. A number of qur'anic verses are interpreted as addressing historical encounters between Muhammad and Jewish communities with whom he came in contact. As recipients of the most recent and final divine revelation, Muslims look back at the earlier monotheistic traditions of Judaism and Christianity as important stages in the full sequence of salvation history. They revere Abraham as a proto-monotheist, a "friend of God," and Islamic tradition associates him with the building of the Ka'ba in Mecca. Moses is a much-revered prophet whose stories occupy a significant portion of qur'anic narrative. The Qur'an recognizes the ancient Israelites as a people chosen by God, who rescued them from their torments and tribulations, such as those they suffered in Egyptian captivity, and who offers his guidance to them through the revelation of the Torah. A summary judgment of this positive assessment can be found in Q 2:62, "Those who believe (in what is revealed to you (Muḥammad), and those who are Jews, and Christians, and Sabaeans—whoever believes in God and the last day and does right—surely their reward is with their Lord, and no fear shall come upon them neither shall they grieve."

Yet the qur'anic depiction of the ancient Israelites also accuses them of idolatry and disobedience. Q 2:54 recounts the episode of the golden calf and Moses' discovery of his people's delinquency. Other verses make accusations of scriptural distortion, Sabbath violation, and usury. The strict food laws of later Judaism are judged to be a consequence of these transgressions: "Because of the wrongdoing of the Jews We forbade them good things which were (before) made lawful to them" (Q 4:160).

This combination of admiration and condemnation also appears in those verses of the Qur'an that are understood as references to the Jewish groups with whom Muhammad had contact during his lifetime. Initially, it was presumed that these Jews would recognize Muhammad as a divinely sent prophet and would accept his message as fully congruent with their own monotheistic beliefs. This proved not to be the case. There was instead strong and active resistance, especially in Medina, where the Prophet assumed political as well as religious leadership. The new Muslim arrivals, as well as their Medinan allies, met this resistance with equally aggressive retaliation, punishing those Jewish communities who conspired against Muhammad and his people. Eventually, the Qur'an posits a sharp contrast between the Jews and the other major monotheistic community, the Christians: "You will find the most vehement of mankind in hostility to those who believe (to be) the Jews and the idolaters. And you will find the nearest of them in affection to those who believe (to be) those who say: 'We are Christians.' That is because there are among them priests and monks, and because they are not proud" (Q 5:82).

A progressive distancing from both Jews and Christians can be charted in the Qur'an as closer association with these groups threw more light on the differences among them than on the commonalities that they share with Muslims. All are subsumed under the label "People of the Book" (i.e., those who claim a divinely given scripture), but the earlier recipients of revelation must now acknowledge the primacy and the finality of the qur'anic message. In political and economic terms, this secondary status is signaled by a tax levied on Jews and Christians: "Fight against such of those who have been given the scripture as do not believe in God or the last day, and do not forbid what God has forbidden by His messenger, and do not follow the religion of truth, until they pay the tribute readily, being brought low" (Q 9:29).

What does the Qur'an say about Christians?

There are verses in the Qur'an that praise Christians and verses that condemn them. But who are the Christians reflected in this qur'anic rhetoric? Scholars have suggested answers to that question, but textual and archaeological evidence for the presence of Christian groups in seventh-century Arabia is scant. We know more about communities of Christians in nearby regions, such as the Syrian desert and southern Iraq or in Ethiopia and the coastal areas of the Red Sea. Yet biographical material on Muhammad speaks of the Christians of

Najran who lived in southwestern Arabia and interacted with the Prophet and his followers.

When the Qur'an mentions Christians it often uses the collective term, People of the Book, meaning religious communities with a divinely revealed scripture. While the term usually comprises Christians and Jews, it can include others. In one instance (Q 5:47), Christians are called "People of the Gospel" (*Injil* in Arabic) but more frequently they are dubbed "Nazarenes" (*al-Nasara* in Arabic), a name that comes from Jesus's hometown of Nazareth. Both the Greek and Syriac of the seventh century use a similar term for referring to Christians.

The qur'anic ambivalence about Christians mirrors a similarly mixed attitude toward Jews, although in a milder form. As just noted, in one famous passage, Q 5:82, Christians are contrasted favorably with the Jews, with the latter being characterized as "the most vehement of mankind in hostility" to the Muslims, while Christians are the nearest to Muslims "in affection." More often, however, Christians are criticized on multiple grounds and Muslims are urged to avoid friendship with them (Q 5:51) and not to fall prey to their efforts to proselytize.

Most criticism, however, centers on theological differences between Christians and Muslims. Three major doctrines create division: the incarnation, the Trinity, and the crucifixion. Since no doctrine in Islam is more central than that of God's singularity or unity, the Christian claim that Jesus is God's son borders on blasphemy for Muslims. Verses such as Q 3:59 underscore the repeated assertion that Jesus is only human and the frequent repetition of the identifying phrase, "Jesus son of Mary," forestall any claims of divinity.

For similar reasons, the Christian doctrine of the Trinity represents another assault on the Qur'an's insistence on God's utter uniqueness. No effort to explain the Trinity as "three persons in one God" and thus fully compatible with monotheism seems to satisfy Muslim theologians, whether classical or contemporary. The imperative expressed in Q 4:171 frequently serves as a rejoinder: "and say not 'Three'—Cease! (it is) better for you!—God is only one god."

The Muslim denial of Jesus's crucifixion invokes a different logic. In the long history of God's sending prophets to human communities, the resistance they initially encounter is eventually rectified through divine retribution against those who oppose the prophet. Prophets are not killed or crucified by their opponents. Their missions prevail and their message triumphs. Q 3:54–55 thus substitutes a crucifixion story with an ascension one. Beginning with a recognition of those who were scheming against Jesus and plotting his death, Q 3:54 reminds that "God is the best of schemers" and that God promises Jesus, "I am gathering you and causing you to ascend to Me, and am cleansing you of those who disbelieve." Commentators on the verse ordinarily fill in the blanks with a scenario in which a criminal is made to appear like Jesus, arrested in his place, and crucified, while Jesus himself ascends to God.

What does the Qur'an say about apostasy?

International news media regularly offer accounts of people being accused of apostasy and even executed or murdered on the basis of such a charge. In Islam apostasy means the active renunciation of one's religion. While it is closely connected with the notion of unbelief or disbelief, it is not the same. The logic of apostasy as a crime builds on the idea that God is infinitely good to humankind and that humans, in turn, are expected to acknowledge God's compassionate goodness and be grateful for it. Disbelief is the rejection of this goodness, either by being ignorant of it or by being ungrateful toward it. The apostate turns unbelief into action by renouncing or withdrawing from a previous state of belief.

The Qur'an recognizes, of course, that some people have no access to God's guidance and are in an original state of unbelief. Apostasy applies to the person who has recognized God and acknowledged his mercy and compassion but then turns away from him. Refusing to live by God's commands and rejecting the guidance God has offered is an even more intensive form of disbelief. Acts of apostasy take different forms, such as denying God's existence or worshipping other gods. Charges of apostasy can be laid against those who curse or mock God or do the same to the Prophet Muhammad. Desecration of holy sites and objects, especially the Qur'an, would also prompt such charges.

Does the Qur'an itself specifically authorize the death penalty for apostates or legitimize their killing? Most scholars would say no, and would point to the hadith as the source of these punishments. Q 9:74 suggests the possibility of repentance but also predicts punishment in this life and the next: "If they repent it will be better for them; and if they turn away, God will afflict them with a painful doom in the world and the hereafter, and they have no protecting friend or helper in the earth."

Q 2:109 even suggests that Muslims forgive those who try to lure them from their faith. The verse points to the situation of "People of the Book" (i.e., Jews and Christians) who try to turn the Muslim believers away from their acceptance and avowal of Islam. The immediately preceding verse, Q 2:108, provides the most succinct characterization of this religious crime: "He who chooses disbelief instead of faith, truly he has gone astray from a plain road."

What does the Qur'an say about blasphemy?

Insulting or showing irreverence for sacred things or holy people does not usually incur criminal charges in the contemporary West, but it can prove lethal in parts of the Muslim world. Blasphemy covers a spectrum of actions and declarations that range from defaming a religion, to vilifying its beliefs and practices, to offending its followers, to mocking its holy persons or places.

The qur'anic term for blasphemy includes more than the ordinary English usage of the term. For example, to deny that the Qur'an is divine revelation or that there will be no day of judgment would be blasphemous declarations. To utter a falsehood about God, such as claiming that God has a son, would fall within the qur'anic condemnation. When Pharaoh declares in Q 79:24, "I am your lord the highest," he is thought to blaspheme.

Later theological and legal literature refined and specified the qur'anic denunciation, cataloguing categories of blasphemy and making the clear connection between blasphemy and apostasy. For a Muslim to mock or deny any of the fundamental doctrines of Islam makes that person an apostate, and apostasy can incur the death penalty. But potentially lethal penalties can be provoked by non-Muslims as well. Further, intra-Muslim charges occur in Sunni-Shi'i relations where Shi'i rejection of the legitimacy of the first three caliphs, Abu Bakr (d. 634), 'Umar ibn al-Khattab (d. 644), and 'Uthman ibn 'Affan (d. 656), invoked charges of heresy and subsequent retribution.

Many countries, both Muslim and non-Muslim, have long had blasphemy laws on the books, although a number have repealed these statutes in recent decades. Sometimes the primary purpose is assuring respect for the majority religion, and sometimes their focus is the protection of minority religious rights. While punishments can range from fines and imprisonment to execution, the latter is true in only a few countries. Among these are Pakistan and Saudi Arabia. Chapter XV of the Pakistan Penal Code details the kind of offenses, such as desecrating holy places or defaming the Prophet Muhammad, for which blasphemy charges can be laid. The charge of defamation of the Prophet, which can incur the death penalty, has been used against Christians and also against groups like the Ahmadiyya, whom most Muslims do not recognize as a legitimate part of the Muslim community. In 2018 the Supreme Court of Pakistan ordered the release of Asia Bibi, a Christian woman who had been sentenced to death by the lower courts for a charge of blasphemy brought against her by Muslim neighbors.

With regard to Saudi Arabia, organizations like Amnesty International and Human Rights Watch have reported cases where Saudi citizens and foreign nationals have been charged with various forms of blasphemy. While imprisonment is the more common punishment, in some instances individuals have been executed. But there are also cases in which the sentences have been appealed and commuted.

In February 1989, Islamic blasphemy laws drew worldwide attention when Ayatollah Ruhollah Khomeini (d. 1989), the Supreme Leader of Iran, issued a formal legal option (*fatwa*) declaring a death sentence against the British author Salman Rushdie. The fatwa stipulated that both Rushdie and his publishers should be executed by any Muslim who was able. Rushdie's crime was the publication of a novel entitled *The Satanic Verses*, which uses dream sequences to provocatively recast key moments in the life of the Prophet Muhammad. Demonstrations against the book in Britain, India, Pakistan, South Africa, and elsewhere erupted into riots during which people died or were injured. International organizations issued statements defending freedom of expression and condemning the death threat, but Rushdie went into hiding and lived for many years under British police protection.

Episodes of Qur'an burning or desecration count as execrable acts of blasphemy in the eyes of believers. The violent backlash prompted by the profanation of the Qur'an at Guantánamo Bay, at a church in Gainesville, Florida, the Dove World Outreach Center, and (perhaps mistakenly) at a US military base in Afghanistan highlights the importance given to proper treatment of the scripture. To repeat yet again that Muslims believe the Qur'an to be the actual words of God makes comprehensible the intense reactions to what is perceived to be unforgivable blasphemy.

What does the Qur'an say about religious tolerance?

The Qur'an says a lot about other religions, especially Judaism and Christianity. These are recognized as predecessor traditions, recipients of divine revelation, and stages in the "salvation history" that finds completion and culmination with God's message to the Prophet Muhammad in the Qur'an. Because they too have scriptures—what the Qur'an calls the Torah (*Tawrat* in Arabic) and the Gospel (*Injil* in Arabic), respectively—Jews and Christians are called "People of the Book." The Qur'an asserts, however, that over the centuries adherents of both traditions have allowed distortions and deletions to compromise their divine revelations, so these corrupted scriptures no longer contain the true revelations originally received.

Nevertheless, the Qur'an accords "People of the Book" a special status within Islamic law. In the early centuries of Islamic history this meant that Jews and Christians could continue in their religious traditions but would have to pay a special tax to the governing authorities. In modern times, this separate and subsidiary status has taken various forms in particular Muslim nations and regions.

In contemporary debates about religious freedom, Muslims regularly invoke two passages from the Qur'an that can be read as commending religious tolerance. The first of these is Q 109 and in its entirety it reads:

Say: O disbelievers!
I do not worship what you worship;
Nor do you worship what I worship.
And I shall not worship what you worship.
Nor will you worship what I worship.
To you your religion, and to me my religion.

Classical and contemporary interpretations of these verses differ. Initially, they were taken to reflect a situation in which the earliest Muslims were begging their Meccan persecutors for clemency. "Don't make us worship your false gods," was the intended meaning. "To you your religion, and to me my religion" was declaring a truce. Now this passage is often used as a qur'anic assertion of religious liberty.

The other passage is Q 2:256: "There is no compulsion in religion. The right direction is distinct from error. And he who rejects false deities and believes in God has grasped a firm handhold which will never break. God is hearer, knower." "No compulsion" means that people cannot be forced to believe. Repeatedly, the Qur'an conveys God's reassurance to Muhammad that all he can do is offer people the message, the divine guidance. God, not the Prophet, instills belief in the human heart.

Reference is also made to the qur'anic recognition of human diversity: "And if your Lord had willed, He would have made mankind one nation, yet they do not cease differing" (Q 11:118). Even religious diversity achieves qur'anic acknowledgment: "For each We have appointed a divine law and a traced-out way. Had God willed He could have made you one community" (Q 5:48). A subsequent phrase in this latter verse has been used as a rallying cry for interfaith cooperation, particularly in joint social justice efforts: "So vie with one another in good works." And its final phrase promises a divine adjudication of religious differences in the life to come: "To God you will all return, and He will then inform you of that in which you differ."

While the historical record reveals that neither Muslim nor non-Muslim countries practiced the kind of religious tolerance that characterizes contemporary secular societies, Muslim governments did offer a protected status to Jewish and Christian groups. Such was not, however, the usual fate of non-Christian groups living within Christian jurisdictions in the same period.

Given the increasingly pluralistic nature of many Muslim societies, especially in Asia and Africa, modern Muslim intellectuals have not surprisingly taken up the concepts of religious toleration and religious pluralism in new ways. Farid Esack in South Africa and Nurcholish Madjid (d. 2005) in Indonesia provide examples of such contemporary thinking. Esack, who was active in the struggle to end apartheid, understands religious pluralism as essential to a fully realized program of social justice. The qur'anic vision of the oneness of God mirrored in the unity of humanity undergirds Esack's insistence on this connection between pluralism and equality.

Living in a country governed by *pancasila*, the fivefold political philosophy that grants official recognition not only to Islam but to Christianity, Hinduism, Buddhism, and Confucianism, Madjid insists that the Qur'an recognizes the natural plurality of human society and that submission to God ("islam" with a small "i") can be fostered through the teachings of Muhammad as well as those of other divine messengers and prophets. The common call to submission creates a single community of all who profess and practice belief in one God and honor the guidance given by God, however conveyed.

RECOMMENDED READING

English Translations

Ali, Abdullah Yusuf, trans. *The Holy Quran: English Translation and Commentary*. New York: Hafner, 1946.

Ali, Ahmed trans. *Al-Qur'ān: A Contemporary Translation*. Princeton, NJ: Princeton University Press, 1988.

Arberry, Arthur J., trans. *The Koran Interpreted*. New York: Macmillan, 1955.

Asad, Muhammad, trans. *The Message of the Qur'ān*. Mecca: Muslim World League, 1964.

Birk, Sandow, illustrator. *American Qur'an*. New York: Norton, 2015.

Haleem, M. A. S. Abdel, trans. *The Qur'ān: A New Translation*. New York: Oxford University Press, 2004.

Irving, Thomas Ballantine, trans. *The Qur'ān: The First American Version*. Brattleboro, VT: Amana Books, 1984.

Khalidi, Tarif, trans. *The Qur'an*. New York: Penguin, 2008.

McAuliffe, Jane, ed. *The Qur'an: A Norton Critical Edition*. New York: Norton, 2017.

Nasr, Seyyed Hossein et al, eds. *The Study Quran: A New Translation and Commentary*. New York: HarperOne, 2015.

Pickthall, Muhammad Marmaduke, trans. *The Meaning of the Holy Koran*. London: Alfred A. Knopf, 1930. For a revision of Pickthall's translation, see McAuliffe (2017) in previous reference.

Sells, Michael A., trans. *Approaching the Qur'ān: The Early Revelations*. Ashland, OR: White Cloud Press, 1999. (Includes a CD with Qur'ān recitations.)

General Introductions and Reference Works

Campanini, Massimo. *The Qur'an: The Basics*. Translated by Oliver Leaman. 2nd edition. New York and London: Routledge, 2016.

Cook, Michael. *The Koran: A Very Short Introduction*. Oxford: Oxford University Press, 2000.

Ernst, Carl W. *How to Read the Qur'an: A New Guide with Select Translations*. Chapel Hill: University of North Carolina Press, 2011.

Esack, Farid. *The Qur'an: A Short Introduction*. Oxford: Oneworld, 2002.

Esposito, John L. *What Everyone Needs to Know about Islam*. 2nd edition. New York: Oxford University Press, 2011.

Gade, Anna. *The Qur'an: An Introduction*. London: Oneworld, 2010.

Kaltner, John. *Introducing the Qur'an for Today's Reader*. Minneapolis: Fortress Press, 2011.

Lawrence, Bruce. *The Koran in English*. Princeton, NJ: Princeton University Press, 2017.

Lawrence, Bruce. *The Qur'an: A Biography*. New York: Atlantic Monthly Press, 2007.

Leaman, Oliver, ed. *The Qur'an: An Encyclopedia*. London and New York: Routledge, 2006.

Mattson, Ingrid. *The Story of the Qur'an: Its History and Place in Muslim Life*. Oxford: Blackwell, 2008.

McAuliffe, Jane Dammen, ed. *Cambridge Companion to the Qurʾān*. Cambridge, UK: Cambridge University Press, 2006.

McAuliffe, Jane Dammen, gen. ed. *The Encyclopaedia of the Qurʾān*. 6 vols. Leiden: Brill, 2001–2006.

Rippin, Andrew, ed. *The Blackwell Companion to the Qurʾān*. Malden, MA: Blackwell, 2006.

Robinson, Neal. *Discovering the Qur'an: A Contemporary Approach to a Veiled Text*. London: SCM Press, 1996.

Siddiqui, Mona. *How to Read the Qur'an*. New York: Norton, 2007.

Sinai, Nicolai. *The Qur'an: A Historical-Critical Introduction*. Edinburgh: Edinburgh University Press, 2017.

Significant Studies

Barlas, Asma. *"Believing Women" in Islam: Unreading Patriarchal Interpretations of the Qur'an*. Austin: University of Texas Press, 2002.

Blair, Sheila. *Islamic Calligraphy*. Edinburgh: Edinburgh University Press, 2006.

Chaudhry, Ayesha. *Domestic Violence and the Islamic Tradition*. New York: Oxford University Press, 2013.

Graham, William A. *Beyond the Written Word: Oral Aspects of Scripture in the History of Religion*. Cambridge, UK: Cambridge University Press, 1989.

Gregg, Robert C. *Shared Stories, Rival Tellings: Early Encounters of Jews, Christians, and Muslims*. New York: Oxford University Press, 2015.

Hidayatullah, Aysha A. *Feminist Edges of the Qur'an*. New York: Oxford University Press, 2014.

Lings, Martin. *The Quranic Art of Calligraphy and Illumination*. London: World of Islam Festival Trust, 1976.

Madigan, Daniel A. *The Qur'an's Self-Image: Writing and Authority in Islam's Scripture*. Princeton, NJ: Princeton University Press, 2001.

Marshall, David. *God, Muhammad and the Unbelievers: A Qur'ānic Study*. London: Curzon, 1999.

McAuliffe, Jane Dammen. *Qur'anic Christians: An Analysis of Classical and Modern Exegesis*. Cambridge, UK: Cambridge University Press, 1991.

McAuliffe, Jane Dammen, ed. *With Reverence for the Word: Medieval Scriptural Exegesis in Judaism, Christianity and Islam*. New York: Oxford University Press, 2003.

Miles, Jack. *God in the Qur'an*. New York: Alfred A. Knopf, 2018.

Nelson, Kristina. *The Art of Reciting the Qur'an*. Austin: University of Texas Press, 1985.

Rahman, Fazlur. *Major Themes of the Quran*. Minneapolis, MN: Bibliotheca Islamica, 1980.

Reynolds, Gabriel Said. *The Qur'an and the Bible*. New Haven, CT: Yale University Press, 2018.

Saeed, Abdullah. *Reading the Qur'an in the Twenty-first Century: A Contextualist Approach*. London: Routledge, 2014.

Taji-Farouki, Suha, ed. *Modern Muslim Intellectuals and the Qur'an*. Oxford: Oxford University Press, 2004.

Tottoli, Roberto. *Biblical Prophets in the Qur'ān and Muslim Literature*. Richmond, Surrey: Curzon, 2002.

Wadud, Amina. *Qur'an and Woman: Rereading the Sacred Text from a Woman's Perspective*. New York: Oxford University Press, 1999.

Online Resources

The following sites offer search capability for the Qur'an by chapter (sura) and verse. Several also provide recorded recitation of the Qur'an verse by verse. For the latter, there are also hundreds of YouTube videos. Dozens of apps for smartphones and tablets are available and the number continues to increase. Use search terms like "quran" and "tajweed" to locate these. Also, several of the English translations in the preceding list are available online.

The Noble Qur'ān: http://quran.com/

Qur'ān Explorer: http://www.quranexplorer.com/quran/

Tanzil Quran Navigator: http://tanzil.net/#1:1

ReciteQuran.com: www.recitequran.com

QuranFlash: http://www.quranflash.com/home?en

These sites have digitized and placed online rare and exquisite manuscripts of the Qur'an, either full or fragmentary.

Chester Beatty Library in Dublin (http://www.cbl.ie/)

Walters Art Museum in Baltimore (https://thewalters.org/)

Museum of Islamic Art in Doha (http://www.mia.org.qa/en/)

Museum of Turkish and Islamic Arts in Istanbul (http://www.kultur. gov.tr/EN-113954/istanbul---turkish-and-islamic-arts-museum. html)

The Agha Khan Trust for Culture and the Massachusetts Institute of Technology maintain a photo archive of major architectural sites, including qur'anic inscriptions, across the Muslim world. (https:// archnet.org/)

INDEX

For the benefit of digital users, indexed terms that span two pages (e.g., 52–53) may, on occasion, appear on only one of those pages.

Aaron, 24
abaya, 154–55
Abbasid dynasty, 106–7
Abbot of Cluny, 125, 142
'Abd al-Malik, 106–7
ablutions, 31, 69., *See also* ritual
    purification
abortion, 157–58
Abraham, 6, 10–11, 24, 46, 47–48,
    49–50, 98, 129, 130, 138,
    158–59, 189–90
abrogation, 10, 115–16, 131, 135,
    156, 168, 172, 178–79, 188–89
Abu Bakr, 12–13, 195
Abu Zayd, Nasr Hamid, 127–28
Abyssinia, 50–51, 79–80
Adam, 39, 43, 44, 47, 49–50, 61, 74,
    91–92, 129, 152
Adams, John, 146–47
adoption, prohibition on, 74
adultery, 73–74, 134, 173–74, 189
Afghanistan, 24, 180, 189, 196
Africa, 159–60, 198–99
afterlife, 36, 52–54, 189., *See also*
    Heaven; Hell; Paradise
age of ignorance, 122–23

Agha Khan Trust for
    Culture, 148–49
ahl al-dhimma, 82–83
Ahmad, Mirza Ghulam, 30
Ahmadiyya, 30, 195–96
Albania, 180
alcohol, 115–16, 135, 167–69, 189
Alexander the Great, 50–51
'Ali, 'Abdullah Yusuf, 163
'Ali ibn Abi Talib, 13, 29, 30, 66,
    115, 118
Allah, 10–11, 37., *See also* God
American Qur'an, The (Birk), 143
Amnesty International, 196
amputation (punishment), 58–59,
    134, 189
amulets, 101
Andalusia, 125
angels, 39, 43–44, 49–50, 53, 54
"Angels, The" (sura), 15–16, 43
Annan, Kofi, 162
annunciation to Mary, 25–26,
    44, 129
Antichrist, 63
apostasy, 17, 127–28, 178–79,
    193–94, 195

Arabian Peninsula, 3, 50–51,
81–82, 126
early Christians in, 191–92
pre-Islamic, 10–12, 157, 158–59
Arabic, 89, 90, 121, 126,
129, 140–42
printing of, 144
reasons for reciting Qur'an
in, 91–92
role of Qur'an in
literature, 137–39
written, 13
Aramaic, 129, 140
Arberry, A. J., 163
architecture, 103–4
Arkoun, Mohammed, 128
art, 103–4
Asia, 198–99
'asr, 64–65
Atlantic Monthly, 13–14
atonement, acts of, 61–62
aural experience of Qur'an, 85–86
ayat, 15–16, 39, 182–83. See also
signs; verses of Qur'an
Azerbaijani translations of
Qur'an, 148
Al-Azhar University, 90, 120,
141, 145
'Azra'il, 53

Baha'is, 82–83
balance (of good and evil
deeds), 62–63
Bangladesh, 68–69, 74–75
al-Banna, Hasan, 175–76
baraka, 101
barzakh, 53
basmala, 15–16, 20
behavior, determinants of, 59–60
Bhagavad Gita, 3
Bibi, Asia, 195–96
Bible, 3, 15–16, 18–19, 26,
49–50, 140, 187–88. See
also Gospel; Hebrew Bible;
New Testament; Old
Testament; Torah
connection between Qur'an
and, 128–30
God of, 37–38
Gutenberg, 143
post-Enlightenment study of,
126, 128
used to understand the
Qur'an, 130–31
Bible, the Qur'an and Science, The
(Bucaille), 136–37
bibliomancy, 100–1
Birk, Sandow, 143
birth control, 158
Black Stone, 69
blasphemy, 35–36, 113, 194–96
blessings, securing of, 100–2
book of deeds, 62–63
Boston Public Library's Rare Book
Room, 146–47
breastfeeding, 73–74
bride wealth, 73–74
Bucaille, Maurice, 136–37
Buddhism, 3, 74–75, 199
Buddhist scriptures, 3, 15
Bulaq Press, The, 144–45
burial practices, 53
burqa, 154–55
Byzantine empire, 11, 50–51, 81–82

Cairo edition of Qur'an, 145
Cairo nilometer, 107
calendars, 6, 67–68
caliphs, 28, 195., See also individual
caliphs
calligraphy, 86, 103–6, 148–49
Canada, 91
capitalism, 184–85
Carlyle, Thomas, 18
ceremonies, formal, 97–98
"Challenge Verses," 116
chapters of Qur'an. See suras
charity, 70–71, 184–85

Chaudhry, Ayesha, 163
Chester Beatty Library, 105, 148–49
child marriage, 74–75
children, 74–75
China, 158–59
Christianity, 19–20, 67–68, 77,
    82–83, 94, 132–33, 134–35,
    172, 174, 181, 182, 189–90,
    194, 195–96. *See also* People of
    the Book
  abortion issue and, 157–58
  child marriage and, 74–75
  Coptic, 81, 82–83
  female genital mutilation
    and, 159–60
  God of, 37–38
  incarnation doctrine, 192
  influence on Qur'an, 126,
    130, 131
  interfaith marriage and, 80, 81
  in Muhammad's time, 11
  qur'anic scholarship in, 125
  Qur'an on, 11–12, 78–80, 81–82,
    83, 190–93
  sexuality and, 160
  Syriac, 126
  tolerance toward, 197, 198, 199
  translations of Qur'an and, 142
  Trinity doctrine, 35–36,
    37, 192–93
Christmas, 67
2 Chronicles, 48
circumambulation of Ka'ba, 69
circumcision, 158–59
Citibank, 185–86
Cluny, Abbot of. *See* Abbot
    of Cluny
coins, qur'anic inscriptions
    on, 106–7
colonialism, 90, 122, 178, 182
commandments, 57–59
commentaries, 112–13, 117–20,
    122–24. *See also* interpretation
    of Qur'an

*Commentary on the Cosmic Verses of
    the Qur'an, A* (al-Najjar), 137
"Common Word between Us and
    You, A" (open letter), 38
community, 76–78, 181
Companions of the Prophet,
    112, 117–18
"Complaint" (Iqbal), 138–39
concubinage, 173–74
Conference of the Birds (al-Din
    Attar), 138
Confucianism, 199
contextualist interpretation of
    Qur'an, 123
conversion to Islam, 80, 170, 174
Coptic Christianity, 81, 82–83
covenants
  between God and humans,
    78, 100
  between Muslims and
    non-Muslims, 82–83
"Cow, The" (sura), 15–16
creation
  of humans, 39, 41–42, 43,
    118–19, 137
  of the world, 38–40, 49–50, 137
crucifixion (of Jesus), 30, 192, 193

Dajjal, 63
Dao De Jing, 3
David, 24, 50, 61, 129, 171
Day of Judgment, 16,
    53–54, 188–89
death, 52–54. *See also* afterlife
death penalty, 189, 194, 195–96
democracy, 179–80
Deuteronomy, 131
devils, 43–44
dhikr, 100
dhuhr, 64–65
al-Din Attar, Farid, 138
"Disbelievers, The" (sura), 15–16
dissenter interpretation of
    Qur'an, 117–18

divine dictation, 23–24, 140–41
divine inspiration, 23, 140–41
divine revelation, 3, 4, 5, 6, 8–9,
    15, 23–25, 47, 128–29
divorce, 73–74, 152–53,
    160, 164–65
"Divorce" (sura), 164
Dome of the Rock, 103–4
domestic violence, 162–63
*Domestic Violence and Islamic
    Tradition* (Chaudhry), 163
Dove World Outreach Center, 196
dowry, 72–74
drug abuse, 168–69. *See also*
    intoxicants

Easter, 67–68
education, 89–91
Egypt, 81, 82–83, 90, 98, 155,
    170–71, 180
Egyptian Council of
    Ministers, 141
Ellison, Keith, 142–43, 145
Emerson, Ralph Waldo, 146–47
end of the world, 62–63
English translations of Qur'an, 18,
    125–26, 142–43, 148
environmentalism, 40, 182–84
Epistles of Paul, 16
Eritrea, 79–80
Esack, Farid, 198–99
Ethiopia, 12, 50–51, 79–80,
    81–82, 191–92
Europe, 91, 92, 96, 126,
    159–60, 180
Eve, 49–50, 61, 74, 129
"Event, The" (sura), 54–55

fajr, 64–65
fasting, 167., *See also* Ramadan
fate, 52–53, 59
al-Fatiha, 101
Fatima, 66
fatwa, 196

female genital mutilation (FGM),
    151–52, 159–60
feminism, 153
figural artwork, aversion to,
    104, 105–6
financial transactions, 184–86
fivefold prayer cycle. *See salat*
food, 165–67
forgiveness, 60–62
fountains, 104
four-wives option, 72–73, 152–53,
    155–56, 173–74
French translations of
    Qur'an, 142–43
Friday (communal prayer day),
    65–66, 97–98
funerals, 98

Gabriel, 4, 5, 15, 23, 28, 43, 44
    Arabic version of name
        (Jibril), 24
    identity of and connection to
        Qur'an, 24–26
Garden of Eden, 47
gender separation, 65–66, 154–55
generosity, 70–71
Genesis, 38–39, 54, 161
genies, 44–45
German translations of
    Qur'an, 142–43
Germany, 123–24
Girls Not Brides, 74–75
Global Qur'an, 148
God. *See also* Allah
    absolute authority of, 177–79
    covenant with, 78, 100
    human behavior and, 59–60
    human relation to, 41–43
    justice of, 186–87
    knowledge of particulars, 133
    love of, 72
    names of, 36
    oneness of, 20, 35–36, 132, 181,
        192, 198–99

of Qur'an and Bible, 37–38
Qur'an as word of, 3–4, 6,
   15, 23–24
Qur'an on, 35–37
Goethe, J. W., 18
Goldziher, Ignaz, 117–18
Goliath, 171
Gospel, 8, 47, 130, 131, 134–35, 197
Gospel of John, 99–100
government, 177–79
greater jihad, 169–70
Great Mosque of Sana'a, 13–14
Greek language, 129, 140
Greek philosophy, 132–33
Greek science, 136
Guantánamo Bay, 31–32, 196
Gutenberg, Johann, 143–44
Gutenberg Bible, 143

hadith, 69, 90, 97, 112, 117–18, 119,
   132–33, 134, 151–52, 165, 194
   on the afterlife, 53–54
   on birth control, 158
   on circumcision, 158–59
   defined, 25
   on end of the world, 63
   explained, 114–15
   false, 114–15
   on jihad, 169–70
   on martyrs, 175
   on Paradise of virgins, 56–57
hafiz, 85–86
Hafsa, 12–13
hajj, 6, 61–62, 68–70, 71, 98
halal meats, 166–67
Haleem, M. A. S. Abdul, 163
Hanukkah, 67
Hasan ibn 'Ali, 66
Hasan II mosque, 103–4
healing, 101
Heaven, 36, 53–56, 62–63, 189., See
   also Paradise
Hebrew Bible, 8, 17–18, 61, 80, 94,
   128–29, 130, 131

Hebrew language, 129, 140
Hell, 36, 52–56, 60, 62–63,
   133, 189
heresy, 125, 127–28, 142, 195
Hidden Book, 27–28
hidden Imam, 71
hijab, 154–55
Hinduism, 80, 199
historical events, 49–51
Homeric epics, 17–18
homosexuality, 161
hostage-taking, 172
houris, 56–57
house of Islam, 170
house of war, 170
House of Wisdom, 136
HSBC, 185–86
Hud, 48–49, 187–88
hudud, 189
human rights, 58–59, 180
Human Rights Watch, 196
humans
   covenant between God and,
      78, 100
   creation of, 39, 41–42, 43,
      118–19, 137
   relation of to God and
      nature, 41–43
Husayn ibn Ali, 175
Hussein, Taha, 127

Iblis, 44
Ibn al-'Abbas, 'Abdullah, 112
Ibn Mujahid, Abu Bakr
   Ahmad, 13
Ibn Sa'id, Omar, 146
Ibn Taymiyya, Ahmad, 131
Ibrahim, Anwar, 161
'Id al-Adha, 69, 71, 98
'Id al-Fitr, 67, 71, 98
idolatry, 104, 135, 190
illiteracy, 6, 19
illumination, 104–6
imams, 90, 97–98, 177–78

incarnation doctrine, 192
independence (from
    colonialism), 90
India, 68–69, 74–75, 90, 180
Indonesia, 68–69, 90, 93, 180
infanticide, 157
inheritance, 75–76, 152–53
inimitability doctrine, 92, 116,
    127, 141–42
Injil, 130, 192, 197. *See also* Gospel
"inquisition" (Islamic), 28
interest-bearing loans, 184–86
international relations, 181–82
Internet, 120, 122, 147–49
interpretation of Qur'an, 111–24
    authority for deciding on
        correct, 119–20
    expert *vs.* nonexpert, 120–22
    modern and
        contemporary, 122–24
    in Sunni and Shi'i
        Islam, 117–20
    verses used for
        guidance, 115–17
In the Shade of the Qur'an
    (Qutb), 122–23
intoxicants, 115–16, 166, 167–69
Iqbal, Muhammad, 138–39
Iran, 82–83, 98–99, 155, 180
Iranian revolution, 180
Iran-Iraq War, 175
Iraq, 31–32, 81–82, 98–99, 126, 175,
    180, 191–92
Irving, Washington, 146–47
Isaac, 24, 47–48
'isha, 64–65
Ishmael, 10–11, 24, 47–48
ISIS, 82–83, 175
Islam. *See also* Shi'i Islam; Sufi
    Islam; Sunni Islam
    conversion to, 80, 170, 174
    growth of in US, 110
    Qur'an shaping of philosophy
        and theology, 132–34

role of Qur'an in
    literature, 137–39
islam (literal meaning of), 177, 199
*Islamic Declaration on Global
    Climate Change*, 183–84
Islamic Foundation for Ecology
    and Environmental Science
    (IFEES), 183–84
Islamic rosary, 36
Islamic Society of North America
    (ISNA), 184
Islamophobia, 31–32
Israel-Palestine conflict, 180
Italian translations of
    Qur'an, 142–43
Italy, 92

Jacob, 24, 47–48
Janissary corps, 174
Jefferson, Thomas, 125–26, 142–43,
    145, 146–47
Jesus, 4, 6, 11, 24, 26–27, 28, 47–48,
    50, 63, 67–68, 130, 192
    birth of, 129
    crucifixion of, 30, 192, 193
    mother of (*see* Mary)
    Muhammad compared
        with, 6–7
    Qur'an on, 37
    Second Coming of, 30
Jethro, daughter of, 72
jihad, 56–57, 169–71
jinn, 39, 44–45
"Jinn, The" (sura), 44–45
"Jizya Verse," 172
Job, 24
John the Baptist, 129
Jonah, 24, 61
Jordan, 180
Joseph, 49–50, 129, 138, 152
Judaism, 67, 77, 82–83, 94, 134–35,
    172, 181, 182, 189, 194., *See
    also* People of the Book
    abortion issue and, 157–58

influence on Qur'an, 126,
130, 131
interfaith marriage and, 80, 81
in Muhammad's time, 11–12
Qur'an on, 11–12, 78–79, 80,
81–82, 83, 192, 194
tolerance toward, 197, 198, 199
justice, 186–87

Ka'ba, 6, 10–11, 53, 69, 189–90
kalam, 132–33
Karbala, 175
Ketton, Robert of, 142, 144–45
Khadija bint Khuwaylid, 4–5
Khalid, Fazlun, 183–84
Khalili, Nasser David, 105
Khomeini, Ayatollah Ruhollah,
178–79, 196
khums, 71
Kinda, 11
King Fu'ad edition of Qur'an, 145

Latin translations of Qur'an, 125,
142, 144–45
Law of the Pseudoprophet Mohamet,
The (Ketton translation), 142
laws/legal issues. See also Shari'a
on circumcision, 158–59
Qur'an on, 57–59, 118, 177–79
legal interpretation of Qur'an,
117–18, 120
Lent, 67–68
lesser jihad, 169–70
Leviticus, 189
Library of Congress,
142–43, 146–47
"Light Verse," 21, 97–98,
99–100, 104
linked commentaries, 112
literature
Qur'an role in, 137–39
Qur'an studied as, 127–28
Lord's Prayer, 19–20
Lot, 161, 187–88

love, 72
lunar calculations, 67, 68

Madjid, Nurcholish, 198–99
madrasa, 89–90, 94–95
maghrib, 64–65
Magian, 83
Mahdi, 63
major ablutions, 31
Majus, 83
Malaysia, 90
Mali, 74–75, 180
Mamluks, 174
Mamout, Yarrow, 146
al-Ma'mun, 28, 136
marriage, 72–73, 74, 98., See also
divorce; polygamy
child, 74–75
interfaith, 80–81, 152–53
between slaves and
Muslims, 173–74
marriage gifts, 164–65
martyrs, 55, 56–57,
151–52, 174–76
Marwa, 69
Mary
annunciation to, 25–26, 44, 129
as only woman named in
Qur'an, 152
sura of, 98
Massachusetts Institute of
Technology, 148–49
al-Mawdudi, Abu A'la, 179–80
Mecca, 3, 136, 181
Christians in, 11
facing during prayer, 65
hostilities between
Medina and, 6
Muhammad's flight from, 5
non-Muslims prohibited from
entering, 69–70
pilgrimage to (see hajj)
suras received in, 9–10,
16–18, 135

Medina, 3, 7, 178, 181
  Christian delegation in, 79–80
  hostilities between
    Mecca and, 6
  Jews in, 11–12, 80, 190–91
  Muhammad's migration to, 6
  non-Muslims prohibited from
    entering, 69–70
  suras received in, 9–10,
    16–18, 135
memorization of Qur'an, 86–87,
    89–90, 94–95
menstrual cycle, 73–74
messengers, 46–47
Michael, 43
Middle East and North Africa
    (MENA), 180
mihrab, 104
Mina, 69
minarets, 65
minor ablutions, 31
miracle, Qur'an as, 116, 141–42
misfortune, prevention of, 100–2
missionary work, 182
modern interpretation of Qur'an,
    117–18, 120
monotheism, 37, 79, 132, 192–93
monotheistic folklore, 27
Morocco, 165, 180
Moses, 4, 6, 26, 46, 47–48, 49–51,
    57–59, 61, 72, 129, 130, 131,
    138, 152, 165, 187–88, 189–90
Mother of the Book, 8–9, 27–28
muezzin, 65
Muhammad ibn 'Abdallah, 7, 19,
    44, 52, 62, 75, 77, 106–7, 111,
    115–16, 117, 121, 128, 140–41,
    168, 174, 176, 178, 181, 199
  appearances of name in
    Qur'an, 46
  audiences of, 130
  biblical foretelling of
    arrival, 131
  birthday commemoration, 22, 98

as both prophet and
    messenger, 46–47
Christians and, 79–80, 191–92
Companions of, 112, 117–18
connection with other
    prophets, 47–49
on Day of Judgment, 53–54
death of, 6
defamation of, 193–94, 195–96
divine revelations to, 3, 4, 5, 6,
    9, 15, 23–25
final message to, 9
as the final prophet, 30
hadith of (see hadith)
human status of, 6–7, 37
illiteracy of, 6
Jews and, 80, 189–91
on justice, 186
knowledge of other
    religions, 10–12
legitimacy of as a prophet,
    27, 47–48
life and impact of, 4–7
poetry and, 21–22
Qur'an following death of,
    12–14, 129
Satanic Verses on, 196
sinlessness of, 109
wives of, 115, 152, 154, 163
mujtahids, 90
Mumtaz Mahal, 148–49
Munkar, 53
Museum of Islamic Art,
    105, 148–49
Museum of Turkish and Islamic
    Arts, 104–5, 148–49
mushaf, 12–13
muslim (literal meaning of),
    78, 177
Muslim Brotherhood,
    170–71, 175–76
Muslim World League, 182
al-Mutawakkil, 107
Muzdalifa, 69

mystical interpretation of Qur'an,
117–18, 120
mysticism, 22, 98–100. *See also*
Sufi Islam

Najaf, 90
al-Najjar, Zaghlul, 137
Najran, 79–80, 81–82, 191–92
Nakir, 53
al-Nasara, 192
Nasr, Seyyed Hossein, 182–83
Nasser, Gamal Abdel,
122–23, 170–71
natural world, 40, 182–84
Qur'an on, 40–41
relation of humans to, 41–43
Nepal, 74–75
Newsweek, 31–32
New Testament, 8, 16, 26–27, 80,
94, 128–29, 130, 131, 140
New Yorker, 17
New York Times, 13–14
Nicaragua, 74–75
Niger, 74–75
Night of Power, 4, 9, 28, 66, 176–77
nilometers, 107
niqab, 154–55
Noah, 24, 47–48, 49–50, 91–92,
129, 187–88
nongovernmental organizations
(NGOs), 74–75, 161
non-Muslims. *See also specific*
religions
marriage to, 80–81, 152–53
prohibition on entering holy
cities, 69–70
Qur'an on treatment of, 78–80
Qur'an studied by, 110, 125–26

occasions of revelation, 10,
115, 168
Old Testament, 128–29, 140
"Opening, The" (sura), 16,
19–20, 97

Organization of Islamic
Cooperation, 182
Owens, James, 146

Pahlavi, Reza Shah, 155
Pakistan, 68–69, 90, 189, 195–96
Palestine, 81–82
pancasila, 199
papermaking, 143–44
Paradise, 41, 52–53, 54, 60, 133,
152, 161, 165, 167–68, 175,
176–77, *See also* Heaven
rivers of, 56
virgins of, 56–57
particulars, God's knowledge
of, 133
patriarchy, 123
peace, 176–77
Peale, Charles Willson, 146
"Pen, The" (sura), 15–16
People of the Book, 11–12, 77, 79,
82, 191, 192, 194, 197
People of the House, 30
Pergamon Museum, 105
Persian empire, 11, 81–82
Persian translations of Qur'an,
111, 141, 142, 148
Peter the Venerable, 125, 142
Pharaoh, 129, 138, 188, 195
Philadelphia Museum of Art, 146
philosophical interpretation of
Qur'an, 117–18
philosophy, Islamic, 132–34
Pickthall, Marmaduke, 18, 19
pilgrimage to Mecca. *See hajj*
Plain of Arafat, 69
Poe, Edgar Allan, 146–47
poetry, 21–22
politics, 177–79
polygamy, 38, 72–73, 152–53,
155–57, 160, 165
Portugal, 92
post-Enlightenment research, 17,
110, 118–19, 126, 128

praise poems, 22
prayer. *See salat*
predestination, 59–60
pregnancy, 73–74, 164
"Preliminary Discourse" (Sale),
    125–26, 142–43
Preserved Tablet, 27–28
profession of faith, 35–36, 52–53
prophets
    appearing in Qur'an, 47–49
    messengers compared
        with, 46–47
prostration (in prayer), 64
protected people, 82–83
punishment, 134, 161, 162,
    187–89, 194
punishment stories, 48–49, 187–88

Qom, Iran, 90, 120
Queen of Sheba, 50–51, 129, 152
Qur'an
    on abortion and birth
        control, 157–58
    advanced degrees in
        study, 94–96
    on angels (*see* angels)
    on apostasy (*see* apostasy)
    arrival in America, 145–47
    art and architecture influenced
        by, 103–4
    on blasphemy (*see* blasphemy)
    calligraphic tradition of (*see*
        calligraphy)
    on charity (*see* charity)
    on children, 74–75
    on Christians (*see* Christianity)
    chronology of, 8–10
    on circumcision, 158–59
    commandments in, 57–59
    on community (*see* community)
    core message of, 132
    on creation (*see* creation)
    on death and afterlife (*see*
        afterlife; death)
    on democracy, 179–80
    descent of, 4, 9, 24, 28, 66
    desecration of, 31–32,
        193–94, 196
    on devils, 43–44
    different parts of, 15–18
    difficulty reading, 18–19
    on divorce (*see* divorce)
    on domestic violence, 162–63
    on drinking and drugs
        (*see* alcohol; drug abuse;
        intoxicants)
    on end of the world, 62–63
    on environmentalism (*see*
        environmentalism)
    as eternal, 27–28
    on fasting (*see* fasting)
    on female genital mutilation
        (*see* female genital mutilation)
    on financial
        transactions, 184–86
    first printing of, 143–45
    on fivefold prayer cycle
        (*see salat*)
    on food, 165–67
    fragments of discovered, 13–14
    on Gabriel (*see* Gabriel)
    God and (*see* God)
    on government and
        politics, 177–79
    on Heaven (*see* Heaven)
    on Hell (*see* Hell)
    historical events in, 49–51
    history and source of, 3–4
    on homosexuality, 161
    on humans (*see* humans)
    illumination tradition in, 104–6
    on inheritance (*see* inheritance)
    inimitability of, 92, 116,
        127, 141–42
    inscriptions from on ordinary
        objects, 106–7
    on international
        relations, 181–82

Internet role in transmission of (*see* Internet)
interpretation of (*see* interpretation of Qur'an)
Islamic philosophy and theology shaped by, 132–34
on Jews (*see* Judaism)
on jihad (*see* jihad)
on jinn (*see* jinn)
on justice, 186–87
law in (*see* laws/legal issues)
literature and (*see* literature)
on love, 72
manuscripts of, 104–6
marginal markings in, 17, 67, 105–6
on marriage (*see* marriage)
on martyrs (*see* martyrs)
meaning of name, 7–8
memorization of, 86–87, 89–90, 94–95
as a miracle, 116, 141–42
Muhammad and (*see* Muhammad ibn 'Abdallah)
mysticism and (*see* mysticism)
on natural world (*see* natural world)
on non-Muslims (*see* non-Muslims)
oral, 15, 92–93
other names for, 8
on other religions, 81–83
on Paradise of virgins, 56–57
on peace, 176–77
on pilgrimage to Mecca (*see hajj*)
on polygamy (*see* polygamy)
prevention of misfortune and securing of blessings, 100–2
on prophets (*see* prophets)
as prose *vs.* poetry, 21–22
in public worship and formal ceremonies, 97–98
on punishment (*see* punishment)

recitation of (*see* recitation of Qur'an)
relative prominence of parts, 19–21
on religious tolerance, 197–99
science and, 136–37
self-referentiality of, 26–27
sensory experience of, 85–87
on separation (*see* gender separation)
on sexuality (*see* sexuality/ sexual relations)
Shari'a and (*see* Shari'a)
showering prior to touching, 30–32
on sin, repentance, and forgiveness, 60–62
size of, 15, 29, 129
on slavery, 173–74
study methods, 89–91
on terrorism (*see* terrorism)
translation of (*see* translation of Qur'an)
variations in for different groups, 29–30
on veiling (*see* veiling)
on war, 171–72
women and (*see* women)
written, 15, 92–93
Qur'an Explorer, 148
Qur'anic Arabic Corpus, 147
Quraysh tribe, 181
Qutb, Sayyid, 122–23, 175–76, 178–79

Rahman, Fazlur, 182–83
Ramadan, 4, 9, 17, 28, 61–62, 66–68, 71, 98, 136, 167, 184
month for, 66
rules of, 66
rationalist interpretation of Qur'an, 117–18
"Recitation, The" (name for Qur'an), 8

recitation of Qur'an, 7, 19, 23, 25,
        89–90, 101
    Arabic as language of, 91–92
    fame for, 92–94
    Internet sites for, 148
reform movement, 7
religious tolerance, 197–99
repentance, 60–62
"Repentance" (sura), 60–61
resurrection, 52, 53–54, 62, 133
riba, 184–85
ritual purification, 30–32, 69
rivers of Paradise, 56
Robert of Ketton, 142, 144–45
Ross, Alexander, 142–43
Royal Aal al-Bayt Institute for
        Islamic Thought, 147
Rushdie, Salman, 196
Ryer, André du, 142–43

Sabians, 83
Sadat, Anwar, 170–71
Safa, 69
salam, 176
salat (fivefold prayer cycle), 19–20,
        64–66, 97
Sale, George, 125–26, 142–43, 145
Salih, 48–49, 50–51, 187–88
Satan, 44, 49–50
Satanic Verses, The (Rushdie), 196
Saudi Arabia, 90, 120, 155,
        189, 195–96
Saul, 129, 171
science, 136–37
scientific interpretation of
        Qur'an, 117–19
seal of the prophets, 6
Second Coming (of Jesus), 30
Second Message of Islam, The
        (Taha), 17
sectarian interpretation of
        Qur'an, 117–18
Senegal, 180
September 11 attacks, 31–32,
        143, 175

Seven Sleepers, 50
sexuality/sexual relations, 66,
        72–73, 160–61
shahada, 52–53. See also profession
        of faith
shahid, 174., See also martyrs
Shah Jahan, 103, 148–49
Shahrur, Mahmud, 121–22
Shari'a, 134–35, 178–79
al-Shaytan, 44., See also Satan
Sheikh Zayed mosque, 103–4
Shi'i Islam, 13, 60, 63, 132–33, 175,
        177–78, 195
    dietary rules in, 166–67
    hadith in, 115
    inheritance regulations in, 76
    interpretation of Qur'an in,
        117–19, 120
    khums of, 71
    Night of Power observed in, 66
    Qur'an version of, 29–30
    ritual purification in, 31
    salat in, 64–65
Shu'ayb, 48–49, 187–88
shura', 178–79
signs, 39, 40, 163, 182–83
sin, 60–62
Six Books, The, 115
slavery, 145–46, 173–74
Smithsonian Institution, 104–5
Solomon, 24, 50–51, 61, 138
Soroush, Abdolkarim, 128, 179–80
Spain, 92, 142, 145–46
stoning, 134, 188–89
Sudan, 74–75
Sufi Islam, 22, 98–100,
        133–34, 169–70
suicide bombers, 151–52, 175–76
sunna, 134, 135
Sunni Islam, 4, 63, 132–33,
        141, 195
    dietary rules in, 166–67
    hadith in, 115
    inheritance regulations in, 76

interpretation of Qur'an
   in, 117–20
Night of Power
   observed in, 66
Qur'an version of, 29–30
ritual purification in, 31
salat in, 64–65
supersessionism, 79, 131
"Sura of Compassion," 39
suras
   longest, 130, 138
   Meccan, 9–10, 16–18, 135
   Medinan, 9–10, 16–18, 135
   names of, 15–16
   number of, 9, 15–16, 29
   ornamental divisions
      between, 106
   textual unity of, 17–18
Surat al-Ikhlas, 21
Surat Yasin, 21
"Sword Verse," 21, 172
Syria, 81–82, 98–99, 191–92
Syriac Christianity, 126

al-Tabari, Abu Ja'far ibn Jarir,
   142
Taha, Mahmud Muhammad, 17
Taj Mahal, 103, 148–49
tajwid, 148
tales of the prophets, 130
Taliban, 189
Tanzil, 148
tasting the Qur'an, 86–87
Tawrat, 130, 197., See also Torah
taxes, 82–83, 170, 191
Ten Commandments, 57–59
terrorism, 65
   Qur'an on, 172
   September 11 attacks, 31–32,
      143, 175
textualist interpretation of
   Qur'an, 123
Thamud, 50–51
theology, Islamic, 132–34
"Throne Verse," 20, 35, 39, 97–98

tombstones, qur'anic inscriptions
   on, 107
Torah, 8, 47, 130, 134–35,
   189–90, 197
touching the Qur'an, 86–87
traditional interpretation of
   Qur'an, 117–18
translation of Qur'an, 18, 111,
   125–26, 144–45
   into European
      languages, 142–43
   Internet sites, 148
   by Muslims, theological
      problem of, 140–42
Trinity doctrine, 35–36, 37, 192–93
tritheism, 37
Tunisia, 156, 165
Turkey, 155, 156, 180
Turkish translations of Qur'an, 142
twelve signs, 53–54

Uhud, battle of, 156
ulama', 90
'Umar ibn al-Khattab, 13, 195
Umayyad dynasty, 106–7
umma, 76–77, 181., See also
   community
umra, 69–70
United States, 159–60, 180,
   184, 189
   arrival of Qur'an in, 145–47
   dhikr in, 100
   dietary issues for Muslims
      in, 166–67
   growth of Islam in, 110
   salat and, 65–66
   study of Qur'an in, 91, 96, 126
   zakat in, 71
Universal Declaration of Human
   Rights, 182
University of Birmingham, 13–14
University of Cairo, 127
University of Chicago, 182–83
University of Jordan, 95–96
University of Leeds, 147

University of Tübingen, 13–14
usury, 184–85
'Uthman ibn 'Affan, 13, 29, 195
'Uthmanic canonical text, 13, 29

veiling, 151–52, 154–55
"Verse of Piety," 20–21
"Verse of Righteousness," 77
verses of Qur'an, 15–16
 clear and ambiguous, 113
 qur'anic interpretation
  guidance and, 115–17
 written on ordinary
  objects, 106–7
"Victory, The" (sura), 181
virgins, Paradise of, 56–57
"virtues/merits of the Qur'an," 21
visual experience of Qur'an, 86

Walters Art Museum, 105, 148–49
war, 171–72
Waraqa, 5
water, 41, 104
wine, 115–16, 135, 167–68
women
 clothing choices of, 160–61

domestic violence
 and, 162–63
female genital mutilation,
 151–52, 159–60
gender separation and,
 65–66, 154–55
inheritance and, 76, 152–53
interfaith marriage and,
 80, 152–53
interpretation of Qur'an
 and, 123
as qur'anic scholars, 94–95
Qur'an on, 152–53
veiling of, 151–52, 154–55
"Women, The" (sura), 152
Women's Mosque of
 America, 65–66
worship, public, 97–98

YouTube, 148
Yusuf Dhu Nuwas, 82

zakat, 70–71
Zaynab, 72
Zechariah, 129
Zoroastrianism, 82–83